WHY WE FOUGHT

INSPIRING STORIES
OF RESISTING HITLER AND
DEFENDING FREEDOM

JERRY BORROWMAN

SHADOW
MOUNTAIN

Interior images: page 3, public domain; page 38, *New York Daily News*, courtesy Camerer; page 71, public domain; page 84, courtesy National Archives UK; page 121, Wikimedia Commons, courtesy Agnes Hirschi; page 144, Roger Viollet/Getty Images; page 169, Wikimedia Commons, courtesy Steve J. Morgan

Visit us at shadowmountain.com

Library of Congress Cataloging-in-Publication Data

Names: Borrowman, Jerry, author.

Title: Why we fought : inspiring stories of resisting Hitler and defending freedom / Jerry Borrowman.

Description: Salt Lake City : Shadow Mountain, [2021] | Includes bibliographical references. | Summary: "Author Jerry Borrowman recounts seven lesser-known stories of World War II spies, resisters, and others who fought for freedom against the Nazi threat"—Provided by publisher.

Identifiers: LCCN 2021013205 | ISBN 9781629729343 (hardback)

Subjects: LCSH: World War, 1939–1945—Biography. | World War, 1939–1945—Underground movements—Biography. | BISAC: HISTORY / Military / World War II | HISTORY / Modern / 20th Century | LCGFT: Biographies.

Classification: LCC D736 .B675 2021 | DDC 940.54/86730922—dc23

LC record available at https://lccn.loc.gov/2021013205

Printed in the United States of America
LSC Communications, Crawfordsville, IN

10 9 8 7 6 5 4 3 2 1

CONTENTS

AUTHOR'S NOTE

Recently a friend asked why I have been so interested in writing about America's involvement in World Wars I and II. It was a fair question, given that *Why We Fought* is my fourteenth published book written about heroic figures who served in the two world wars. After thinking about his question for a moment, I replied to my friend that since childhood I have been fascinated and inspired by the courage of ordinary men and women who risked their lives on behalf of freedom. It is worthy to fight for your country—but so much more meaningful to fight for an ideal, like liberty.

In the case of the seven stories featured in *Why We Fought*, most fought on behalf of the Allies even though not required to do so— they were volunteers in defeating Nazi Germany and the horrible repression it represented. All of them were at constant risk, yet they persisted because it was the right thing to do.

Which brings me back to my friend's question—I write about these people because their stories deserve to endure, and they should be honored by as many readers as possible. Quite simply, we should never forget. Thank you for sharing in this experience.

CHAPTER 1

VIRGINIA HALL

"WE MUST FIND AND DESTROY HER"

INTRODUCTION

Report to OSS London on two days of sabotage in Nazi occupied France, August 4, 1944:

"A bridge blown at Montagna; an automobile road cut and four cuts in the railroad near Langogne; a German freight train derailed in a tunnel near Brassac; a German freight train derailed in a tunnel near Bioude; a railway bridge blown near Le Puy; the Monistrol D'Allier freight train derailed in a tunnel and 15 meters of track destroyed in Solignac; a railway bridge destroyed at Lavoute; a railway bridge wrecked at Chamalieres and the locomotive driven into the gulf below; 500 newly recruited French resistors organized into companies."[1]

These activities were done under the direction of Virginia Hall in her role as leader of the Heckler Circuit, one of the largest resistance networks in France. It was a remarkable accomplishment, particularly since many of the French Maquis (freedom fighters) were not at all used to the idea of reporting to a woman. But through sheer competence and extraordinary bravery she proved herself more than equal to the challenge of directing millions of francs and hundreds of thousands of pounds of supplies, guns, and ammunition dropped by parachutes into the hands of those locals brave enough to run the risk of Nazi retribution to help free their country from German domination.

Those who reported to Virginia in 1944 knew her only as "Diane," the code name assigned to her by the United States Office of Strategic Services (forerunner to the Central Intelligence Agency). But a small handful in Washington and London knew the true identity of the woman whom the Nazi Klaus Barbie, the infamous "Butcher of Lyon," identified as "the Enemy's Most Dangerous Spy." In wanted posters distributed throughout France he added, "We Must Find and Destroy Her." With a price on her head, Virginia Hall was never safe. Even more remarkable, this was her second time in France. The first time she worked as an operative for the British; the second time, she worked for the United States.

LEADERSHIP AT AN EARLY AGE

Though it would be decades before her heroism in World War II was posthumously made known to the world, her leadership skills came as little surprise to her fellow students at the Roland Park Country School in Baltimore. After all, they elected her class president, editor-in-chief of the school newspaper, and captain of the field hockey team, recognizing her courage and charm from an early age. But Virginia displayed an unusual style of leadership; one day she wore a live snake to school as a bracelet; she hunted with a rifle, rode horses bareback, and otherwise did her best to live up to her classmates' description of her as the "most original" among them. Virginia's father was a successful Baltimore banker, her mother a socialite who relished circulating among Maryland's social elite. Her mother had great plans for her daughter to marry into money and maintain the family's prominence into the next generation. But Virginia was far too restless for that. Despite attending some of the most prestigious universities in America, including Radcliff College, Barnard College, and George Washington University, she always dropped out before completing a degree. At Barnard she failed physical education simply because she didn't show up for class. But despite those failures she showed remarkable skill in languages, eventually learning to speak French, German, Spanish, Italian, and Russian in addition to her native English. Much to her later regret she always had an American accent when speaking these languages, which increased her risk of detection while fighting the Nazis.

Virginia moved to Paris in 1926 at age twenty and then to Vienna in 1927 to complete her academic studies at the Konsular Akademie, where she studied languages, economics, and journalism. After Virginia received her degree, Virginia's mother hoped that her daughter would come home to Maryland and settle down, but Virginia was just getting started on her remarkable life in international affairs. Her next move was to join the US State Department with an initial assignment in Warsaw, Poland. She was assigned as a consular service clerk—that was the most that a young woman could achieve at the time. But Virginia had high hopes of one day advancing into the diplomatic corps, where she would have real influence and authority. Though it would be difficult, a narrow path was open if she could pass the required competency tests.

Her dreams of a career at State were dashed, however, after a hunting accident on December 8, 1932. Having transferred to Smyrna, Turkey, from Poland, she quickly made friends with associates at the embassy as well as local contacts. She was invited to go bird hunting, and, on the outing, Virginia was carrying a loaded 12-gauge shotgun when she came to a wire fence. Lifting her leg to pass over, she got tangled in the wire and fell forward, and her shotgun discharged directly into her left foot. The pain was staggering; in just a few moments she passed out. Her friends quickly applied a tourniquet and then rushed her to the hospital. The pellets were removed from her foot and, though the accident was severe, the doctors felt that she would make a full recovery. And she did, for approximately three weeks. Then, a few days before Christmas, her condition worsened as a deadly infection set in, followed by gangrene that began crawling its way up her left leg. On Christmas Day 1932, a surgeon was called in to amputate her left leg just below the knee. It was the only action that could save her life. But it was to have far-reaching consequences to her dream of advancing in the State Department diplomatic corps.

The amputation had the immediate effect of pushing the usually exuberant Virginia Hall into an emotional depression as she tried to imagine the future without the use of her leg. Fortunately, the gangrene was arrested and her wound began to heal. But the ordeal was not over. On January 5, 1933, a new infection took root in the sutures that enclosed the stump of her leg below the knee. Soon she was delirious from the pain as the doctors in the Smyrna hospital tried frantically to arrest the infection. Virginia's life hung in the balance.

It was in this precarious condition that Virginia had a remarkable experience that was to influence the rest of her life. In her fevered state, Virginia believed she had a vision of her deceased father appearing at her bedside and telling her that she must not give into the pain and that it was her "duty to survive." He then went on to promise Virginia that if the pain became truly unbearable, he would come back for her, but that he hoped she would endure. This was a turning point, and despite the odds against her survival, Virginia prevailed as the infection slowly subsided. From that point forward Virginia Hall believed that her dead father had come to her rescue by encouraging her to fight to live, and that in doing so he had given new purpose to her life.[2]

Eventually Virginia returned to Baltimore to continue her recovery while living with her mother. It was here that she was fitted with a hollow wooden prosthetic leg with an aluminum foot, which she named "Cuthbert." This prosthetic and its successors were both a boon and a bane for the rest of her life. A prosthetic enabled her to walk and to ride a bicycle, but it was often a source of pain where the stump of her leg joined to the artificial limb, separated only by a sock to absorb moisture—and sometimes even blood when she overexerted herself. Plus she was condemned to walk with a limp, which was one of the identifying characteristics that the Nazis would later use in their attempts to discover her identity and capture her.

When Virginia was finally able to return to service at the State Department she was again assigned as a consular service clerk with a transfer to Venice, Italy. In 1937 she sought permission to take the qualifying tests to advance into the diplomatic corps. But this time her request was rejected because of a State Department policy that read:

"The regulation governing physical examinations to the Foreign Services prescribe that amputation of any portion of a limb, except fingers or toes . . . is a cause for rejection, and it would not be possible for Miss Hall to qualify for entry into the Service under these regulations."[3]

Virginia could continue as a staff secretary but could never hope to pursue her dream of becoming a diplomat. She did not give up her dream easily—appeals were made by prominent friends and politicians on her behalf, eventually reaching President Franklin D. Roosevelt himself. But when Roosevelt asked Secretary of State Cordell Hull if an exception could be made for Virginia, the Secretary took umbrage at her lobbying efforts and said it would be "unseemly." There were no further appeals available. So in May 1939, while at her post in Tallinn, Estonia, Virginia decided that she must resign from the State Department to pursue new dreams for her now-uncertain future. After packing her bags and saying her goodbyes, she traveled to Paris to console herself with the companionship of friends in the French capital.

It was a consequential decision, for it was in Paris that she was to find her new passion and a new and even more exciting way of living her life than she could ever have imagined.

GERMANY ATTACKS FRANCE

World War II started on September 1, 1939, when German forces invaded Poland. Two days later France and Britain declared war on Germany in accord with their mutual defense treaty with Poland. As an American citizen Virginia was free to return home, but she decided to stay in her adopted France.

After months of inaction by both the French and German armies leading into the winter and spring of 1940, Virginia and a friend, Claire la Tour, decided that they should do something to help. So, they enlisted in the *Services Sanitaires de l'Armee* (French Army Health Services) to become ambulance drivers. They received four weeks of training in first aid, which included applying tourniquets and dressings, as well as basic self-defense moves in case they were physically attacked while in the field. Their first assignment was to the city of Metz near the German border, placing them very near the front lines when Germany launched its "Lightning War" against France on May 10, 1940. Within a matter of days Virginia's life was overwhelmed with blood and suffering as she worked long into the nights ferrying wounded French soldiers to field hospitals and occasionally to the permanent hospital in Metz. It was grueling, emotionally draining work as she witnessed firsthand the pain and terror of injured soldiers who were overmatched by Germany's ferocious attack that advanced all the way to Paris in just six weeks.

The casualty count was staggering. For example, in the early morning hours of May 30, 1940, Virginia completed three trips to the hospital before 9:00 A.M. Later that morning, on her fourth trip, she came across the bloody remains of a French soldier who caught her attention. He had taken a bullet to the face, leaving him unrecognizable except for a photo in his pocket. It was her best friend Claire's brother. Now she and Claire felt firsthand the loss of a loved one to the ravages of war.[4]

Virginia's work as a driver was particularly difficult because of the strain of operating the clutch of the ambulance with her prosthetic leg for hours on end. The stress tortured her left hip and her stump was frequently left bleeding and sweaty. Still, she worked all hours of the day and night to help—even acting as a nurse when her ambulance ran out of gasoline. As the Germans made their inexorable march toward Paris, Virginia shared the misery of the French soldiers and peasants whose homes and cities had been overrun by the relentless and ruthless advance of the German army.

On June 13, 1940, Paris was declared an open city with a promise to the Germans that they could enter the city peacefully with no resistance. The next day German tanks rolled into the great city with a massive display of military might and a promise to occupy France as a "protector." The government of France fled to the south, and on June 19 petitioned Germany for an armistice. This was granted with approximately two-thirds of northern France under military occupation by Germany for the duration of the hostilities with Great Britain. A provisional French government for the unoccupied areas of the country was established in the small town of Vichy, with Marshal Philippe Pétain of World War I fame as its new leader. This government formed a shotgun alliance with Germany, promising to supply food, men, and matériel to assist the German war effort. In turn, Germany would cease military action against France.

Virginia was still in the field helping to deal with thousands of injured men and civilians when the capitulation occurred. In time, she made her way back to Paris. Still a worker in the *Services Sanitaire*, she worked in a local hospital helping injured soldiers to recover. But she was disturbed when she realized that as soon as they were healthy enough to travel, these soldiers would either be sent to one of eighty prison camps in France or to Germany to work as slave laborers in military production.

Virginia was indignant, and she desired to find a way to join a resistance group to fight against the Nazi occupiers. But she could not find any groups to join. So in August 1940 she decided to make her way to London. With no direct travel between occupied France and England, she took a train to neutral Spain and then booked steamer passage to London. It was on the trip to Spain that she had a fateful encounter—one that would turn her into one of the most successful clandestine operatives in military history.

THE SPECIAL OPERATIONS EXECUTIVE (SOE)

While traveling by train to Irun, Spain, Virginia was befriended by a stranger who introduced himself as George Bellows. From his accent she gathered that he was British. During their 400-mile train trip the two shared stories of their contempt for what the Nazis were doing to the French people as Germany exploited French resources to support their war efforts. Bellows was impressed when he learned that Virginia spoke six languages, and he marveled at her courage when she told him about her experiences as an ambulance driver.

At the border with Spain, the two separated as Virginia descended so she could walk through the passport control office. Her American passport was in good order, but she wondered how Bellows would get through if he was, indeed, British. She was surprised when, on the Spanish side of the border, he somehow materialized next to her and asked if she would like to join him and some of his friends for dinner that night. It was a large group of both Spanish and British men and women. As she was departing the party, Bellows handed her a note with some names written on it. He said they were friends of his in London that she "ought to look up." The next morning Virginia boarded another train for the Atlantic coast and was in London several days later.

Once in London she put the note from Bellows away and forgot about it. She presented herself to the American embassy as a former State Department employee and asked for a temporary job while she waited to return to the United States. Her linguistic abilities drew the attention of the military attaché, who needed a secretary, and soon Virginia was back at work. Her arrival in the autumn of 1940 put her squarely in the path of the Blitz, Germany's bombing campaign against major British cities including London. Thus, she had already faced the Germans as they invaded France and now, a second time, as the Luftwaffe attempted to bomb the British capital into submission.

It was a vicious onslaught. Germany bombed London for fifty-seven consecutive nights attempting to destroy British morale. The goal was to force England to seek an armistice in advance of Germany's planned attack on Russia. The worst attack came on December 29, 1940, when the Luftwaffe dropped more than 10,000 incendiary bombs on London, destroying the historic city center. In all, more than 18,000 tons of bombs were dropped on the city while Virginia was in residence, causing 28,000 civilian deaths. Yet she never complained and seemed to feel it her duty to share the hardships of those who were fighting the hated Nazis. To the Nazis' dismay, their air campaign paradoxically *strengthened* British morale and the citizens' resolve to support Winston Churchill's war government, and so the bombing came to an end.

In December 1940, Virginia applied for travel back to the United States to take up her life there, expecting that she could travel at State Department expense. But because she had more than a year's break in service, the request was denied. Since there was virtually no civilian travel available, she found herself stuck in London with no chance of advancement or of doing anything to really hurt the Nazis. That is when she recalled the note from the man she met on the way to Spain.

There are differing accounts of how she was recruited by the British Special Operations Executive (SOE). The SOE was a clandestine British agency created by Winston Churchill shortly after the outbreak of war with the intent of creating chaos behind German lines by enlisting the aid of freedom-minded local citizens. It was based on the 1920s agitation created by Irish separatists, who had shown that a well-organized resistance of hostile citizens could harass and demoralize a well-organized army. In one account of Virginia's recruitment, she called the phone number on the paper given to her by Bellows and reached Nicholas Bodington, a former Paris-based, ex-Reuters newspaper correspondent who was now working in London at the F-Section of SOE (which was responsible for espionage in France). In this account Bodington invited Virginia to his home and was fascinated as she explained that, as she could not now return to America, she wanted to return to France to help the people revolt against the Nazis.

Bodington listened without giving away his position or interest, but he was very interested! F-Section had tried unsuccessfully for six months to infiltrate an agent into France, and here was a woman with experience in the country who was practically volunteering for the job. The next morning, he brought her name to the attention of his superior at F-Section, Maurice Buckmaster, with a strong recommendation that they enlist her help. The fact that she spoke French with a strong American accent could be turned to their advantage by sending her into Vichy France as a newspaper correspondent for a friendly American newspaper. Although no one at SOE had thought about using a female agent, they recognized an opportunity when they saw it and invited Virginia in for a recruiting interview.

In the second version of her recruitment, it is said that Virginia had contacted many of the people on Bellows list and become friends with them. She was invited by this group to a party at the home of Vera Atkins, a London socialite who was said to work at the "war office." When Vera asked Virginia what she thought of the Nazis based on her experience in Paris, Virginia responded quickly with contempt followed by examples of Nazi brutality to Jews and ordinary French citizens. She ended by saying that she would like nothing better than to return to France to take on the "filthy" Germans. She even said that she had heard that Quaker groups in America were being allowed into France on goodwill missions and that she might use that as cover to return to France. Vera Atkins said nothing but reported to F-Section the next day that Virginia might be worth recruiting. A call was made to Virginia inviting her to have lunch with Vera a few days later. When Virginia returned the call, it was answered by the "Inter-Services Research Bureau," the cover name for the SOE. It was to this group that Virginia was recruited.

However it was that the invitation happened, Virginia met all these characters: Bodington, Buckmaster, and Vera Atkins. When presented with the opportunity of switching employment to the British with the opportunity to return to France to gain intelligence she accepted without hesitation. After ten years of struggling without success to enter America's diplomatic corps, she was now given an opportunity by the British. On February 17, 1941, she became an operative of SOE. She would be the first agent to enter France with the task of establishing a resistance movement.

The next step was to teach her the tools of the trade of spycraft, espionage, and sabotage. For this she was sent to an estate southwest of London where she was to be trained on "demolition, field craft (clandestine survival), Morse code, weapons training, map reading, canoeing, parachuting, bomber receptions, security, and the general organization of an underground circuit."[5] It was a grueling course of study that required both physical and mental stamina. Virginia loved the weapons training and worked hard to keep up with her instructors in all areas in which the recruits were challenged.

After three weeks she passed the first round and was sent to Scotland for more difficult field training, including use of automatic machine guns, knives, map reading, and deciphering enemy tactics. She was given explosives training for blowing up bridges and other vital infrastructure. She and the others in her group learned how to use plastic explosives to destroy railways. And in one memorable session one of her instructors told the group that they should never kill a German; it was better to wound him since that would send him to the hospital where the Germans had to care for him—a dead soldier was soon forgotten, but an injured soldier required attention and resources. In other words, it was all about tying up the Germans and reducing their ability to fight.

The trainees also did a great deal of hiking, which was difficult for Virginia and Cuthbert, her artificial leg, but she never complained and never slowed the group down. At times, her stump was bloody at the end of the day, but she endured and persisted. Perhaps the most important part of her training was to develop a personal story for her fake identity and to practice it until it sounded natural and unrehearsed. Her public name in France was to be Brigitte LeContre, an American journalist working for the *New York Post*. Her code name was Germaine, by which all escaping British airmen who turned to her for help would call her, as well as other operatives who needed her assistance when in her sector. Virginia worked hard to get her story down—harder after being summoned to a basement in the middle of the night, where faux Gestapo agents questioned her ferociously, even throwing a bucket of ice water at her when they didn't like her answers. But Virginia stuck to the script perfectly, and in so doing passed the last requirement for graduation from basic training. Out of twelve women who started the program, Virginia was one of just two who completed it. She was ready to go to France.

AN AMERICAN IN . . . LYON

Virginia arrived legally in Vichy France posing as a reporter for the *New York Post* on August 23, 1941, having entered the country through Spain. She immediately introduced herself to Vichy officials to establish her credentials as a reporter. In doing so she made friends with Suzanne Bertillion, the chief Vichy news censor, who agreed to introduce Virginia to mayors, industrialists, and other politicians in central France to provide stories for her newspaper articles. Virginia later recruited many of these people to help in her resistance efforts. Her next move was to the city of Lyon, where she formally started her reconnaissance work for the SOE, reporting on the morale of French citizens living under Nazi rule.

Vichy France was depressing. President Pétain had made it clear his government intended to work with the Nazis. He had established a quasi-police force known as the *Milice* (militia) who were responsible for turning in citizens suspected of clandestine work. Members of the Milice were every bit as vicious in their treatment of French citizens as were the Gestapo and Abwehr (German military intelligence) working in the area. Torture and starvation were the tools of their trade—even against their fellow countrymen. The thought that motivated the Milice was that since it was so obvious that the Germans would win the war against England, leaving France permanently under the Nazis' thumb, it made sense to cooperate and gain favor rather than to antagonize the Germans. That is why in 1940 and 1941 so few locals were willing to help in resistance efforts. It also explains why so many among the citizenry were willing to betray their neighbors who *did* choose to join the fight to reestablish French freedom.

Another problem that troubled many of the French was that a huge influx of refugees had entered central France from neighboring countries at the outbreak of war, overwhelming French resources and leaving food and fuel in short supply. This irritated the locals while leaving thousands of displaced persons struggling. Many of these refugees were anti-Nazi and willing to do anything to thwart their domination. These competing forces made Lyon a hotbed of resistance activity—as well as anti-resistance action by the Milice.

Finally, as the war moved to the Mediterranean, increasing numbers of downed British aviators were crossing through central France hoping to make it to neutral Spain and from there return to England. These men needed help and shelter to make their escape.

Thus the battle lines were drawn between the Vichy French (and their German overseers) and the locals and refugees who were committed to casting off German rule. It was into this environment that Virginia soon immersed herself, always on the side of the resistance.

For example, once established in Lyon, Virginia's social skills enabled her to begin building a robust network of supporters. While she eventually had hundreds of individuals working for her, the following are some of the most prominent. The role they played in her network demonstrates the kinds of activities she fostered.

Dr. Jean Rousset was a local gynecologist who hated the Nazis—so much so that he even certified some local prostitutes as free of venereal disease when they were not, thus infecting the Nazi officials who used their services. After an encounter where a British agent became so frightened that he failed to respond to a Milice question even though he spoke fluent French, Virginia stepped into the conversation and told the inquisitor that he was mentally incapacitated. This excuse was accepted, and the Milice withdrew in some alarm.

This gave Virginia an idea, and at her suggestion Dr. Rousset built a mental asylum on an upper floor of his practice, ostensibly to treat people suffering from insanity. But its true function was to provide a safe place for escaping prisoners and refugees, since the local French *and* Germans alike were disinclined to go near what was then known as an insane asylum. Dr. Rousset also provided free medical care to the people Virginia and her network assisted, including operatives who came in by parachute or boat from England. Rousset had a bright and cheerful personality and was fiercely loyal to Virginia, often putting himself at great risk to help her.

Robert LeProvost, who had worked for the French intelligence services for many years, helped Virginia find printing presses willing to print forged identity cards for escaping British airmen as well as forged ration books. He was particularly invaluable to the network because of his extensive contacts with members of the local police (*gendarmerie*) who were sympathetic to the cause. The *gendarmes* often provided advanced warning of Milice raids or could look the other way when strangers showed up in town.

Germaine Guerin was the wealthy owner of a successful Lyon brothel. She provided financial assistance to Virginia's network as well as crucial intelligence gleaned by the women who worked for her in their interactions with their German and Vichy clients. Guerin also used her establishment to provide temporary housing for those moving through Virginia's escape network. She and Virginia became great friends and collaborators.

George Whittinghill, the American vice-consul stationed in Bordeaux, allowed Virginia to use his diplomatic pouch to get messages securely out of France and into American hands, where vital information could then be transferred to London. Although this method was slower than using wireless transmissions, there were times when it was the only means of communication the British had with their field operatives in all of France because of intensive

German surveillance of wireless broadcasts. The Germans sent range-finding trucks out into the countryside to triangulate where illegal radios were operating and then burst in and arrested the operators and seized the equipment. Operators of illegal radios were almost always tortured and then killed.

Jean and **Marie-Louise Joullian** owned a factory in the French town of LePuy, which they used to shelter escapees and to provide them with money.

Marcel Leccia accepted perhaps the most dangerous assignment of all. He successfully infiltrated the *Sûreté*, a police force that specialized in discovering British agents and torturing them until they revealed details of the French and British operatives who helped them. Having Leccia inside this group gave Virginia an ally inside the enemy camp, and it was crucial to her survival to have this access since the Germans and their French collaborators were extremely successful in finding and destroying British-led resistance efforts. It is almost impossible to overstate the danger she faced. Of 119 SOE agents sent to France during World War II, only fifteen survived.[6] It was remarkable that, given the extent of her network and the length of time she stayed in France, Virginia was one of those fifteen.

What exactly did Virginia Hall and her network of agents do? Here is a partial list of the types of intelligence-gathering activities she supervised, as recorded in her SOE personnel file in London:

Despite the mounting dangers, she was collecting details of the political situation in France; the scope and effect of Vichy propaganda; the use of dummy wooden aircraft to fool British aerial reconnaissance; the identity and movements of German regiments; the warring factions within the French Resistance; the installation of machine gun nests on the flat roofs of Paris; and lists of possible sites for future sabotage attacks that would reduce the need for aerial bombing raids with their inherent dangers of civilian deaths. Through what she called her "political information service" (composed of both serving and former officials she had cultivated), she was able to provide London with vital revelations on Vichy relations with the Axis powers. These included reports on top-secret meetings between Pétain and Hermann Göring (Hitler's deputy), and Count Ciano (Mussolini's son-in-law) with Admiral François Darlan (Pétain's deputy), intelligence almost certainly sent to Winston Churchill himself.

She reported on "the 'temper' of the French people, notably how many were dismayed by Britain's humiliating surrender to the Japanese in Singapore . . . and the fiasco of the escaped 'Channel Dash' German battleships" in February 1942. "The French are 'still hoping for their [British] victory and many, many of them are willing to help,' she noted, 'but they would appreciate seeing something concrete besides retreating.'"[7]

Virginia reported on conditions in multiple ways. First, she filed stories with the *New York Post,* which helped her maintain her cover. Few of these articles were openly critical of Vichy, since to do so would get her deported. The only exception was when she wrote about the cruel and inhumane treatment of Jews, many of whom Vichy officials betrayed to the Germans for deportation to concentration camps while treating them all as substandard persons without full rights—even those who had been French citizens for many generations. Virginia also used the diplomatic pouch to send out requests for supplies, money, and to provide information on landing zones, safe houses, and reliable contacts for those who entered the country. Some transmissions to London included requests for weapons. And, after she was given her own "pianist" (a Morse code operator), she filed reports directly with London using the code names assigned. All these activities helped SOE prepare a large underground paramilitary force that was prepared to rise up when the Allies ultimately invaded France.

But Virginia was doing far more than simply gathering

intelligence. She became a central point of contact for anyone passing through the Lyon region. For example, British agent Peter Churchill spoke extensively of the numerous times Virginia helped him as he established himself in the area. When Churchill first arrived in Lyon, he was very hungry and without any meal tickets. When he finally connected with Virginia twenty-six hours after arriving, she took him to a black market restaurant operated by a friendly owner who gave them a sumptuous meal not available to those living on meal tickets.

On a later mission he was frustrated when one of his contacts refused to help him arrange the escape of ten prisoners from a nearby French prison. When he confessed his frustration to Virginia, she scoffed at him, saying, "Is that all?" She asked how much money he had for the operation to which he replied, "Anything up to a million francs." Her reply, "Child's play—what do they think we do out here? Consort with princes and high society? Why, there isn't one of us who hasn't got at least a couple of unscrupulous lawyers up his sleeve who would jump at a crooked assignment like that. If these prisoners are held in Marseille, Olivier will handle it for you. He's an expert at such transactions, and I'm a little too busy on a similar proposition in Lyon to take it on just now."

She quickly arranged for Churchill to meet Olivier, who took the money and made the arrangements. With that simple support from Virginia his impossible mission was solved, and the prisoners were freed. With nothing left to do in France he asked her to send a coded message to London indicating that he would soon make his way to Barcelona. She easily made the arrangements, just as she handled dozens of similar escapes during her time with the SOE.[8] On another occasion Virginia traveled with Churchill to Marseille by train to reduce questions about him—a man and woman traveling together aroused less suspicion than a lone stranger—and to use her local knowledge to prevent him from making an error.

Errors were a constant threat; for example, one British operative was quickly arrested shortly after arriving in France when he requested butter for his bread roll at a restaurant; butter was all sent to Germany at that time. Another was nearly betrayed when he ordered alcohol with his meal on the wrong day—the French were only allowed this luxury every other day. So to protect Churchill from making a fatal blunder, Virginia went along to help him properly acclimate to the dangers he faced.

On this trip to Marseille, after a great deal of walking, Churchill asked Virginia about her prosthetic leg, later writing, "I was struck by the speed and ease with which my companion walked. I said to her, 'Is it true about your foot, Germaine [Virginia's code name]?' 'Yes,' she replied, smilingly, 'it's actually made of aluminum, and there's an opening where it fits round the heel.' 'Good heavens!' I exclaimed, 'A walking ground-floor letter box that nobody would ever find. Hermes had nothing on you, Germaine.' 'You're right,' she replied. 'You'd be surprised at what goes into my aluminum puppy.'" They laughed and found their way to one of the many cafes in Marseille where she had a relationship with the owner.[9]

On their final occasion together, Virginia helped Churchill arrange a hurried escape across the Pyrenees mountains to Spain. In his memoir after the war Churchill wrote the following about Virginia: "After many hours and two changes, we reached Perpignan. It was bitterly cold, as it had been everywhere else. In fact, if there was one thing that I would remember better than any other about this whole venture, it was that I had felt like an icicle most of the time. . . . This, however, did not prevent Germaine from being the most genial of companions, and she never complained about anything."[10] When it was time for them to say goodbye, Churchill said, "I took her hand and said: 'I don't know what I should have done without you, Germaine. What with your cheerful company, your good judgment, and your visits to the chemist's shop to cure my jittery innards, these five or six days have been raised from their bare grimness to a period for which I shall always be grateful to you. . . . Thanks for everything, and *au revoir.*' The train started to move. The whistle blew and she climbed the steps, pulled down the window and looked out. '*Au revoir,*' waved Germaine. There was gratitude and affection in my answering wave."[11]

Churchill's experience with Virginia Hall is indicative of the gratitude felt by hundreds of men and women who met and worked with her. She was unflappable in the face of danger, but impatient with incompetence. She fostered a sense of belonging and loyalty that was unusual and profound. More than one of her group who were later captured and interrogated by the Germans endured intense torture and pain rather than betray their friend and protector, Virginia Hall.

After her last encounter with Peter Churchill, the time for her departure was fast approaching. Because of the extreme danger they worked in, London ordered its operatives to return home after six months in the field to "cool off." But Virginia was deemed so essential that she spent more than fifteen months in France, the danger of her being captured increasing each day. By now the Nazis and Milice both knew that there was a foreign-born "limping woman" integrated into the resistance effort. As her network grew to many hundreds of supporters, the risk of betrayal grew. In August 1942 she worked with twenty-five SOE operatives, six "pianists," and coordinated activities with eight other cells in France by organizing multiple airdrops comprising more than a ton of supplies. It was impossible for the Germans *not* to know that this was happening— they just didn't know who was coordinating it.

And then Virginia and her network were placed in great peril by SOE London. They asked her to meet a Catholic *abbé* (abbot) from Paris, Robert Alesch, who was working behind the scenes to assist the SOE. Virginia was highly suspicious of Alesch when she met him because of his mannerisms and inquisitiveness about matters that did not concern him. But he had the proper credentials and provided help to her on several important projects. Still, she kept her distance, refusing to introduce him to other members of her circuit, even as he pressured her to do so. She was wise to stand back from Alesch, for time would show that he was a double agent secretly working for the Nazis.

In the late fall of 1942, the American embassy in Vichy notified Virginia that the American invasion of North Africa was imminent, and that it was likely that Germany would formally occupy Vichy France as a result. They advised her and all other Americans living in France to leave the country. Still, she delayed for two weeks while frantically trying to help others escape, and while fortifying her network for their work after her departure. By this time Klaus Barbie, a senior Gestapo agent, had arrived in Lyon and had begun a merciless and disturbing campaign to root out all resisters. He singled out the unknown "limping lady," saying that "I would give anything to get my hands on that limping Canadian [expletive]." This indicates that the Gestapo knew that the leader of the resistance was a North American woman, but obviously did not yet realize it was the woman *they* knew as Brigitte LeConte from the United States.

Klaus Barbie was a sadist who found perverse pleasure in torturing his prisoners. Among his favorite techniques of inflicting pain was to pull out a person's fingernails; to press down on the nerve of a shattered tooth; to burn a prisoner's skin with a cigarette (or soldering irons or acid); to nearly drown a person in an ice-cold bathtub; and occasionally, if a woman was Jewish, he'd simply smash her face with his jackboot. He often did this while stroking the fur of his pet cat. History has named him the "Butcher of Lyon" and labeled him as a sadistic murderer responsible for more than 4,300 killings. It was Barbie who was furiously looking for Virginia Hall. It was he who put out a wanted poster identifying her as the "The Enemy's Most Dangerous Spy: We Must Find Her and Destroy Her!"

Fortunately, Robert Alesch had not yet figured out that Virginia was the woman the Gestapo was looking for, and he still did not know the identity of the key members of her circuit. So he was not ready to betray her circuit yet, because he felt he could identify even more members before bringing her down. This gave Virginia a very narrow window in which to escape. On the evening of November 10, 1942, she was warned by a friend at a restaurant that the Nazis were arriving that very evening at midnight to occupy all of France. Virginia caught the last train to Perpignan, near the Spanish border, at 11:00 P.M., literally with just an hour to spare.

ESCAPE ON FOOT THROUGH THE PYRENEES

After leaving the train in Perpignan, Virginia proceeded on foot to the small town of Lavelanet. She bargained with a contact there for a guide to take her and three others across the mountains. The price was 55,000 francs. Her first night was spent in a safe house, where she asked the wife of her guide for an additional sock that she could use to separate Cuthbert from her stump. The woman was sympathetic and gave her the sock as well as some precious salve.

At midnight Virginia and her companions started their climb into the mountains. The next few days were grueling and cold. In the dead of winter, Virginia had to negotiate a steep mountain path through snow that made it difficult to use her prosthetic leg. At times she had to maneuver precariously across rocky crags on narrow ledges many thousands of feet above the valleys below. By the end of the first night she had climbed more than 4,000 feet to a pass at 8,071 feet. The others in her group were exhausted by the effort, at least one wanting to turn back because of the strain. Yet Virginia made it with a prosthetic leg. Once at the peak they descended into a sheltered valley where their guide led them to a snow-covered cabin. Inside he built a fire and gave them hot food and four hours to sleep. Virginia applied salve to her stump and changed the sock, then strapped on her leg for the next part of the journey. They set off again on November 12th to climb to another pass at 7,847 feet. Virginia accomplished this while dragging Cuthbert much of the way because it was simply too difficult to maneuver in the snow.

On their second night they reached a small village, still in France, where a young family had straw for them to sleep on. Virginia was also able to use a shortwave radio to contact London to tell them her whereabouts and that she had three others with her. That set them to work preparing contacts for her in Spain. When London asked if there was anything else, she replied, "Cuthbert is being tiresome, but I can cope." There was a moment of silence and then London radioed back, "If Cuthbert is tiresome, have him eliminated."[12] London thought Cuthbert was one of her companions. For the first time in several days Virginia had a good laugh.

On the third day they descended into Spain where the weather moderated, and the worst of the trek was over. On November 13, 1942, they arrived at the small town of San Juan de las Abadesas where Virginia paid the guide the second half of his money (the first half was held in escrow back in France) and thanked him for his care. Fortunately, Spanish was one of the six languages Virginia spoke, so she was confident she could maneuver on her own. The group split up to prearranged guest houses. But the next day Virginia and her group made the mistake of arriving early at the train station, where locals recognized them as strangers. Even though Spain was neutral, the government of dictator Generalissimo Francisco Franco arrested anyone entering the country illegally. The group was reported to the Spanish Civil Guards, who arrested them.

Virginia was taken to a prison in Figueras, where she spent the next twenty days until the American consul in Madrid could arrange for her release. Once she was safely in Madrid, preparations were made for her to return to London.

What Virginia could not know, at that time, was that back in Lyon, France, Robert Alesch had spoken with Virginia's maid, indicating that Virginia was in great danger and that he had to reach her immediately. The alarmed maid had no idea of Virginia's true role or whereabouts so she told Alesch that he should reach out to Madame Germaine Guerin for help in locating Virginia. With this contact in hand, Alesch began the systematic unwinding of Virginia's network. He had been a double agent all along, being paid handsomely by both the British and the Germans.

The most prominent members of Virginia's network were arrested and made available to the barbarous Klaus Barbie. He tortured all of them, but Dr. Jean Rousset got the worst of it. He was tortured mercilessly while being shown a sketch of the "limping lady" whom he knew to be Virginia, but he refused to betray her. Barely surviving the ordeal, Rousset was sent to the Buchenwald concentration camp in Germany. Another of Virginia's assistants, Eugene Jeunet, was arrested, interrogated, and then suffocated while being transferred to prison. All these freedom fighters were betrayed by a priest who claimed to be their friend.

FROM THE SOE TO THE OSS

Almost as soon as she reported to SOE headquarters in London, Virginia started agitating to be reinserted into France. But Maurice Buckmaster insisted that it was too dangerous. Instead, she was transferred to Madrid, where she assumed cover as a correspondent for the *Chicago Times*. Her real activity was to set up safe houses for those escaping into Spain from France and to help them find their way to safety. She was highly effective at this activity, though bored at being out of the real action. When two members of her circuit, Marcel Leccia and Elisee Albert Allard, managed an escape to Spain, she connived with them on how they could return to northern France as a team to start a new circuit there. Her letter to Buckmaster requesting yet again a transfer to France is a great example of Virginia's personality, assertiveness, and drive:

"I've given it a good four months [here in Spain]. Anyhow, I always did want to go back to France and now I have had the luck to find two of my very own boys here and send them on to you. They want me to go back with them because we worked together before and our teamwork is good. Besides, we have a lot of contacts that—well they will explain it to you. I suggest that I go back as their radio, or else as aider-and-abetter, as before. I can learn the radio quickly enough despite skeptics in some quarters. When I came out here [to Spain] I thought that I would be able to help F section people, but I don't and can't. *I am not doing a job. I am simply living pleasantly and wasting time. It isn't worthwhile and after all, my neck is my own, and if I'm willing to get a crick in it because there is a war on, I do think . . . Well, anyhow, I put it up to you.* I think I can do a job for you along with my two boys. They think I can too, and *I trust that you will let us try, because we are all three very much in earnest about this bloody war.* My best regards to you and the office."[13]

It was not to be. Buckmaster was adamant that the danger was too great. What Virginia did not know at that time is that a competitor agency of the SOE, British MI6, had allowed one of its operatives to give the Gestapo Virginia's true identity so he could protect his status as a double agent. Virginia was known by name and was on Germany's equivalent of its most-wanted list. So Buckmaster insisted she remain in England.

Soon Virginia returned to London to debrief returning operatives and to train new agents going into France. To ease her frustration as well as to recognize her unique contribution, Virginia was made a member of the Most Excellent Order of the British Empire. The award is known as an MBE and was a rare honor for an American woman. Although Virginia was entitled to receive the award directly from King George VI, she declined because she felt it important to preserve her anonymity so she could somehow get "back in the game." But no transfer came, and Virginia was miserable.

That was about to change. Through her extensive network of friends, she learned of a new American spy service, the Office of Strategic Services (OSS). A friend who knew all about it arranged a meeting between Virginia and William "Wild Bill" Donovan, the swashbuckling head of OSS who was in London at the time, staying at the luxurious Claridge Hotel. Donovan had earned his nickname in World War I when he yelled at a group of men under his command, "What's the matter with you—you want to live forever?" while urging them into battle.

Franklin Roosevelt had created the OSS with the charge to connect with resistance groups behind enemy lines to carry out subversion, guerilla activities, and sabotage. But America was late to the game and had not successfully set up a network in France. Virginia was just what Donovan was looking for, and he was the right person for her. She quit her job at SOE and started a new career working for her native country in the OSS with instructions to establish a new network in France. Virginia Hall was back in the game!

MASTER OF DISGUISE

By this point Virginia was not naïve enough to think that she could return to France as she had before, having learned that her identity had been compromised by MI6. So she went to the OSS costume department and received special training on how to disguise herself. As in most other things, Virginia became an undisputed master of this art. While preparing to leave Portsmouth for a secluded beach in Normandy on March 20, 1943, she changed into her new identity—that of an elderly French woman with gray hair, tattered clothing, and a shuffle that disguised her limp. She wore only clothes that had been recently smuggled out of France so that they would be authentic. She even went so far as to have the fillings in her teeth replaced with the type of fillings used by the French. When she showed up at the motor torpedo boat, the men she had been traveling with did not recognize her! Virginia had transformed herself into a new person. Her OSS code name was "Diane."

Virginia's initial charge was to help another agent set up a network operating out of Paris. After a few days in Paris at the home of a friend, she moved out to the countryside to the village of Crozant, where she went to work for a local farmer. He provided her a small cottage with no running water or electricity and she worked for him milking cows, churning butter, and selling cheese. It did not take long before she turned cheese-selling into intelligence gathering through selling cheese to passing German Army officers. As they stopped at her booth in the village, they chatted with each other in German, not knowing that the elderly French vendor spoke fluent German as one of her six acquired languages. Through this eavesdropping she picked up vital information to pass back to OSS London by wireless.

A new problem arose when a German unit stopped at her cottage and searched it high and low for a wireless set. Fortunately, Virginia had hidden her radio cleverly enough that it was not discovered. But the Germans did find fresh cheese in her house and asked to buy it. When the officer in charge stepped forward to pay her, he remembered meeting her in the village. Now that her living place was known, Virginia realized that this was too close of a call. Obviously, the Germans had detected her broadcasts and would eventually close in. She requested permission to move back to Paris.

After a brief time in the city, she moved to the town of Cosne near her old haunts in Lyon. She became a boarder in the home of the local chief of police, Colonel Vessereau, and his wife, who were members of the resistance. In 1942 few Lyon residents wanted to join the resistance because Germany was clearly dominant. But in 1944, the tide had turned with Germany being driven from North Africa and in a fight for its life in Russia. As a result, far more people were willing to sign up to resist the Nazis. Once Virginia gained Colonel Vessereau's confidence, he told her that he had well established contacts within the local Maquis, a group of young men who went into hiding early after the German conquest of France to avoid being sent to Germany as slave laborers.

The Maquis lived off the land as best as possible and were anxious to fight the Germans—but they had no arms or explosives. It was the perfect opportunity for Virginia to set up her own new network, codenamed "Heckler." While her successes while working for the SOE in Lyon at the outbreak of war were impressive, her success as head of OSS Heckler would be spectacular!

Her first decision was to split the Maquis up into groups of twenty-five each and to keep their assignments isolated from the other groups so that if someone was captured by the Germans he could not give up anyone beyond his own group. Next, she radioed OSS London that she needed supplies. On May 15, 1944, they sent cargo aircraft to drop supplies in by parachute, including plastic explosives, magnetic firing devices, and incendiaries to start fires. Soon, Virginia became known to many resistance units in the area and they came calling for help in getting supplies from London. From her initial post as a farmer's assistant selling cheese, she now had a central role in arming thousands of men and women who were anxious to help France rid itself of the hated Nazis.

As June 1944 approached, no one in France knew when the cross-channel invasion would take place. But London did, and they were willing to drop massive supplies of ammunition, guns, explosives, money, and everything else needed to disrupt Nazi supply lines and interfere with Nazi troop movements to the Normandy beaches.

Things moved very quickly; within less than a month Virginia was in command of thousands of resistance fighters, all poised to act when the Allies made a move against the Germans stationed in France.

Perhaps *command* is the wrong word for Virginia's role. While she did go into the field to support missions of sabotage and destruction, her primary role was to distribute Allied supplies only to those groups who agreed to take orders from OSS London. Her second role was to act as a Morse code operator, sending wireless communications to OSS London about Nazi positions, troop movements, and to request the supplies for the various groups willing to help. Thus, while she was not the equivalent of a general sitting atop the command structure of an army, she had incredible power by virtue of her ability to distribute war supplies to a selected resistance group or to withhold them. When a group chose to work with her it was to carry out her instructions to destroy a specific bridge, attack a specific ammunition supply depot, or ambush a known German troop movement. If a group wanted to do things their own way, they received no support from the Heckler Circuit. It was in this way that Virginia became one of the most powerful women in France on the eve of D-Day, 1944.

JUNE 5, 1944—ONE OF JUST THIRTY-THREE AMERICANS IN FRANCE

It's incredible to believe, but on the night before the D-Day landings in Normandy, there were just thirty-three Americans in France. That number would swell into the millions in the coming weeks and months. The greatest advantage the Allies enjoyed on D-Day was that their landings occurred where Germany did *not* expect them to land. Their greatest danger was that Germany could quickly rush troops, tanks, and munitions to the forward areas once the landings occurred. It was this threat that the resistance units all over France were supplied to address. Those resistance forces, including Virginia's Heckler Circuit, were to provide the Allies with real-time intelligence on German movements and activities. They were also tasked with convincing massive numbers of French citizens who had cowered under Nazi rule to step forward and assist them in driving the Germans out of France. And they were to cause chaos and terror among the German troops stationed in vulnerable positions throughout the country to destroy their morale. Virginia was superbly suited to the task before her.

But until the Germans were rooted out, she was in constant danger of discovery and immediate execution. Because she acted as the radio operator for her unit, far from American lines, the Germans were constantly using their rangefinders to attempt to identify wireless broadcasts and destroy them. That is why Virginia was forced to move three times in as many weeks. No place was safe for the wireless operators who transmitted through public airwaves for the supplies and war matériel that were used to harass the Germans.

In June 1944, in the weeks after the D-Day landings on June 6, the sabotage of the German Wehrmacht (army) took place far behind enemy lines. By July, the Germans were in retreat and Heckler was able to step up its activities as increasing supplies rained down from the skies. With these supplies and saboteurs trained by Virginia and others of the OSS and SOE, they destroyed railroad tunnels, blew up bridges, derailed freight trains, attacked German trucks, and destroyed ammunition dumps. For example:

On July 29th, eighteen men attacked a convoy of seven German troop trucks and captured 135 men, killing fourteen Germans.

On August 8th, the villages of Le Puy and Yssingeaux were "in a state of siege and all northeast and west approaches to Le Puy were out. Most of the Tatar[14] troops conscripted by the Germans in the area deserted to the Maquis."[15]

On August 19th, the village of Le Puy was captured with fifty German trucks and 800 German soldiers trapped.

On August 20th, "Diane" signaled that the Haute Loire section of eastern France was cleared of all German troops, and she requested further instructions.

On August 23rd, the remains of a German convoy surrendered at Estivareilles. Five hundred prisoners were taken and all were treated in accordance with the Geneva Convention.[16]

Virginia Hall had arrived in France in March 1944. Five months later, on August 25, 1944, the Allies entered Paris and France was once again a free nation. Virginia's assigned sector to the southeast of Paris had been cleared of Germans two days earlier. In a moment of triumph, Virginia had worked herself out of a job.

POSTWAR

In the last days of the fighting Virginia met a young Frenchman by the name of Paul Goillot, who became her second-in-command. He was lively and funny and clearly interested in Virginia. The two soon fell in love and became partners. As the Allies advanced across the Rhine into Germany there was talk that Hitler was taking an elite group of SS guards to his hideout at Berchtesgaden, Austria, to make a last stand. Virginia and Paul volunteered to go there to disrupt his plans and received authority and training to do so. But on the day they were supposed to go, word was received that the operation was off. Hitler had committed suicide and the war was coming to an end.

At the end of the war Virginia returned to Lyon to learn the fate of her friends from her days working for the SOE. They had paid a terrible toll, but she was grateful that many survived. Dr. Jean Rousset had survived Buchenwald but returned a broken man. Though downcast, he managed a smile for Virginia when she showed up at his door. He filled her in on many of the others. When she expressed guilt for leaving them, he shushed her, saying that all who supported her had fully understood the risk and were glad to have had her help in what was, after all, a French fight for the soul of their country. As she moved on to her many other surviving friends in the area, their stories were almost always the same—they had been brought in for cruel interrogations, followed by arrest and transport to prison camps. When they returned home after hostilities ceased, they found that their houses had been plundered by the Nazis, with anything of value stolen. For example, after sending Madame Guerin to prison, they stole everything from her business and her beautiful home, including expensive and rare artwork, precious carpets, and even the plumbing from inside the walls. But she, like many others, had survived and was grateful to be alive. Virginia sorrowed for their suffering and mourned for those who had died. But she was grateful for the chance to reunite as friends.

After a year of traveling throughout postwar Europe on behalf of the OSS to gain intelligence on the Communists, Virginia returned to the United States with Paul at her side and reported to OSS headquarters there. Shortly thereafter the OSS was transformed into the Central Intelligence Agency (CIA). In the years that followed Virginia always had a job, but only a few overseas assignments that put her in the field. While Virginia often agitated for a field position to resist Communism in Eastern Europe, her style of clandestine work fell out of favor and she was not fully appreciated by the male-dominated culture at the CIA in the postwar years. Still, in 1956 she became the first woman appointed to the CIA's career staff.

Paul started a restaurant. He and Virginia married on April 15, 1957. They had a happy life together, enjoying entertaining many guests, including old friends from their days in the OSS. They purchased an estate in Virginia, which Paul cared for after selling his restaurant. Virginia retired from the CIA in 1966 when she reached the mandatory retirement age of sixty. She died on July 12, 1982, and Paul followed five years later.

AWARDS AND HONORS

Virginia often called herself a "woman of no importance," and she eschewed public recognition for her work. She always had it in the back of her mind that she would go undercover again and so did not want her face known to America's enemies. But, the governments she served were grateful: She received the *Croix de Guerre* (Cross of War) with Palms from the French Government, the Distinguished Service Cross from the United States (declining an audience with President Harry Truman), and the MBE (Order of the British Empire) from the United Kingdom. After her death, these three governments united to pay special tribute to Virginia by commissioning a painting of her sending a Morse code transmission by wireless, assisted by one of the men who supported her in the Heckler Circuit operating a hand-turned crank to provide electricity for her wireless set. This painting was presented to her niece at the home of the French ambassador to the United States, Jean-David Levitte, who was joined by the British ambassador, Sir David Manning. Manning gave her niece, Lorna Catling, a copy of the warrant signed by King George VI when she received the MBE in 1943 and Levitte presented a letter from French President Jacque Chirac commending Virginia's bravery in helping their country achieve independence. Her OSS DSC citation provides a neat summary of Virginia's service after she returned to France in 1944:

> Memorandum for the President from William J Donovan Regarding Distinguished Service Cross (DSC) Award to Virginia Hall, 05/12/1945: SECRET
>
> Miss Virginia Hall, an American civilian working this agency in the European Theater of Operations, has been awarded the **Distinguished Service Cross** for extraordinary heroism in connection with military operations against the enemy.
>
> We understand that Miss Hall is the first civilian

woman in this war to receive the Distinguished Service Cross.

Despite the fact that she was well known to the Gestapo, Miss Hall voluntarily returned to France in March 1944 to assist in sabotage operations against the Germans. Through her courage and physical endurance, even though she had previously lost a leg in an accident, Miss Hall, with two American officers, succeeded in organizing, arming and training three FFI Battalions which took part in many engagements with the enemy and a number of acts of sabotage, resulting in the demolition of many bridges, the destruction of a number of supply trains, and the disruption of enemy communications. As a result of the demolition of one bridge, a German convoy was ambushed and during a bitter struggle 150 Germans were killed and 500 were captured. In addition, Miss Hall provided radio communication between London Headquarters and the Resistance Forces in the Haute Loire Department, transmitting and receiving operational and intelligence information. This was the most dangerous type of work as the enemy, whenever two or more direction finders could be tuned in on a transmitter, were able to locate the transmittal point to within a couple of hundred yards. It was frequently necessary for Miss Hall to change her headquarters in order to avoid detection.

Inasmuch as an award of this kind has not been previously made during the present war, you may wish to make the presentation personally. Miss Hall is presently in the European Theater of Operations. **William J. Donovan Director**. Declassified[17]

The Central Intelligence Agency also reevaluated Virginia's status after her death and highlighted her accomplishments within the organization. Today she is one of just five employees of the CIA to have a special section in the CIA Museum celebrating her exploits. The other four are all former directors of the CIA, and Virginia is the only woman. Virginia's niece donated the painting of Virginia to the CIA, where it hangs in a prominent location in the lobby. In 2016 the CIA named a building after her. Perhaps the greatest honor of all is that all CIA operatives learn about Virginia in their training program, a tribute by the CIA as well as a means of elevating the status of women who serve. Certainly, no one is more deserving of such recognition and respect.

CHAPTER 2

WILLIAM SEBOLD AND SABOTAGE IN AMERICA

INTRODUCTION

On January 11, 1917, a saboteur's incendiary pencil ignited a flash fire at the Canadian Car and Foundry Company in the New Jersey Meadowlands, just seven miles from New York City. The fire led to the destruction of 275 thousand 3-inch explosive shells as well as a huge supply of TNT and other munitions that were destined for World War I allies fighting against Imperial Germany. The fire lasted for four hours, successive explosions rolling across the Meadowlands as more than 1,400 employees fled the scene. The fire and explosions completely destroyed the factory and all its contents, with total damage of $17 million (the equivalent of $372 million in 2020).[1] An investigation in 1927 proved that the perpetrator of this sabotage was a German agent, Fiodore Wozniak, who worked at the factory. But Wozniak escaped prosecution in a plea agreement wherein he agreed to testify against Franz Von Papen, a member of Kaiser

Wilhelm's general staff (and later vice-chancellor to Adolf Hitler), whose agents had recruited Wozniak to the secret service. Wozniak disappeared after testifying.

Then in the summer of 1941, Wozniak appeared again, offering his services as a saboteur to the Anastase Vonsiatsky spy ring operating in New York City on behalf of the Nazi regime. When asked what sort of things he could do in behalf of the Fatherland, Wozniak pulled out a list of chilling incidents that had occurred in America in the previous few months: On January 10, 1941, the British freighter *Black Heron* burned on a Brooklyn pier while taking on a cargo of Douglas dive bombers; on January 20th, a fire swept through two wings of the Navy Department building in Washington, DC; two days later a mysterious fire broke out in the Philadelphia Navy Yard, and two days after that a Navy administration building burned to the ground in Norfolk, Virginia. In February there had been four major fires at munitions powder plants. In May naval piers and railroad yards on both the East and West Coasts caught fire, including a devastating fire on May 31 at the Jersey City waterfront that caused $25 million in damage. In early June, multiple fires broke out at the Cramp Shipyard in Philadelphia. A high-speed passenger train was derailed near Pittsburgh, with five passengers killed and more than 100 injured—the wreck occurred in an area known to harbor Nazi sympathizers.[2] It was a devastating trail of destruction that Wozniak seemed to relish.

When it was suggested that the fires may have been accidental, Wozniak said he knew the cause—sabotage—and even offered the names of those who had perpetrated many of the acts. Now he was volunteering to do even worse, using the latest technology Germany could produce to wreak havoc on the war industries in the United States. For example, in addition to the incendiary pencils, in which the lead in a pencil was replaced by two chemicals that would start a fire when mixed, there were now explosive devices that could be placed in canned vegetables being sent to Great Britain that would kill everyone within twenty feet when punctured by a can opener. The Germans had also developed chemicals infused into envelopes that would explode when the recipient opened the letter. Wozniak said he was capable of these and even greater acts of terror, if given the resources.

The Ukrainian priest to whom Wozniak was applying was well connected within the underground Nazi network active in the United States. What Wozniak could not know is that the priest was also an informant to the Federal Bureau of Investigation. While the FBI would not move against Wozniak for many months, waiting to see who else he collaborated with, they were able to tie him up with phony espionage work rather than unleashing his talents for deadly sabotage.

While the vast majority of American citizens with ties to Germany were loyal to the United States, Wozniak and thousands of other American-born or naturalized citizens were part of a "fifth column"[3] that operated within the United States in the years leading up to World War II. Their goal was to steal American military secrets and to ignite a campaign of sabotage and terror. One of the most direct ways they aided Germany's war effort was to gain information on military aid being shipped to England and to pass that intelligence along to U-boats at sea. This led to ships and lives being destroyed by torpedoes and vital war materials going up in flames or sinking to the bottom of the ocean.

Fortunately, there were those who secretly helped the FBI to identify and deflect these groups, ultimately leading to the collapse and arrest of all the major German spy rings in the months between September 1941 and August 1942. This chapter tells the story of one particularly brave man who, though born in Germany, took very seriously his oath on becoming an American citizen:

"I hereby declare, on oath, that I absolutely and entirely renounce and abjure all allegiance and fidelity to any foreign prince, potentate, state, or sovereignty, of whom or which I have heretofore been a subject or citizen; that I will support and defend the Constitution and laws of the United States of America against all enemies, foreign and domestic; that I will bear true faith and allegiance to the same; that I will bear arms on behalf of the United States when required by the law; that I will perform noncombatant service in the Armed Forces of the United States when required by the law; that I will perform work of national importance under civilian direction when required by the law; and that I take this obligation freely, without any mental reservation or purpose of evasion; so help me God."[4]

In doing so, he placed his own life in peril, as well as the lives of his mother and siblings who still lived in Germany. He was, in many regards, America's first World War II hero, even before America entered the war.

WILLIAM SEBOLD COMES TO AMERICA[5]

Gottlieb Adolf Wilhelm Sebold was born in the city of Mülheim, Germany, in 1899. He served in the German Army in World War I, serving for eight months in the infantry on the dreaded Western Front of the Somme. Living conditions in the German trenches during the last months of the war were appalling as soldiers suffered from malnutrition, infectious diseases, and mustard gas attacks. Perhaps worst of all, Sebold was infected with the 1918 Spanish flu and spent the last months of the war in a military hospital. The effect of these maladies was lifelong ill health for Sebold.

After the war, Sebold decided to act on his penchant for adventure. At twenty-three he signed on as a seaman aboard a merchant ship bound for Galveston, Texas. Once in America, he jumped ship and went looking for a job using the Americanized name of William Sebold. But after just a year away from home, his mother pleaded with him to return to Germany to help the family through the economic crisis that had swept across the Ruhr Valley following Germany's defeat in World War I. Once back home he spent a year working in Germany and helping to pay down the mortgage on his mother's home. He then set off for South America to find new fortunes. In Chile he was hired as a diesel specialist for a mining company, then he moved to California where he worked in both the aircraft and mining industries. With the onset of the Great Depression he moved to New York City, where he connected with the large German immigrant community.

There were many German clubs and "bunds" (federations) in Manhattan that advocated for German-American citizens as well as provided social events. It was in this setting that Sebold met and married Helen Buchner in 1931. Five years later, on February 10, 1936, Sebold took the United States oath of citizenship. It was an oath he refused to break. Shortly after that he moved with his wife to Southern California, where he went to work in an airplane factory. But the dry air adversely affected his health and after a few years the couple moved back to New York. His wartime ill health continued to dog him, and he was eventually hospitalized for severe stomach trouble.

COERCED BY THE NAZIS, SEBOLD RETURNS TO GERMANY

In the fall of 1939, Sebold decided to travel to Germany to visit his family and to recuperate in the familiar climate of the Ruhr Valley. His wife did not join him on the trip. After an uneventful passage on a Hamburg-America steamship he arrived in Hamburg, Germany, where he was surprised by questions asked of him in the passport control office. Specifically, officials asked about his time working in aircraft factories in America. The fact that they knew he had worked in these factories suggested that it was already known to the authorities that he was traveling to Germany—and that they were interested in what he could tell them. Sebold had little to say, since his work in the factories had limited intelligence value. Nor was he inclined to betray his new country. Still, he was told to expect a future visit from unnamed officers and was then allowed to proceed to his mother's home in Mulheim-on-Ruhr.

For the first few months he rested while recuperating from his stomach surgery the previous year. Then, in the summer, he felt well enough to take up work at a steam turbine factory. While America was still in the Great Depression, Germany was secretly rearming for war, so industry was booming. This work gave Sebold enough money to help his mother pay down her mortgage and meet other necessary expenses. With nearly four months behind him he hoped that the prediction that he would again be visited was forgotten. But he received a letter one day signed by a Dr. Gassner asking him to meet for lunch. When they eventually met, Gassner started asking him detailed questions about airplane manufacturing in the United States and whether Sebold had worked on a special bombsight that the Americans were said to be developing for heavy bombers. Sebold replied honestly that he had not seen any bombsights, that he was a skilled laborer who only worked on the specific parts of an airplane assigned to him.

Even so, Gassner told him that the *Abwehr* (German military intelligence) and the Gestapo wanted him to return to America as one of their agents to conduct espionage assignments on behalf of the German people. Sebold said no, later telling the FBI that he told Gassner, "If you want to find out, go there yourself—it is a wide-open society," to which Gassner referred to "the funeral clothes they'd give me when I was stretched out there."[6] Sebold now realized the risk to his life if he refused, so he tried to stall.

"'There's only one question in my mind,' said Sebold, 'and that is whether I would be adaptable enough to such work to be of real service to you.'

"'Of course, you would be very successful,' said Gassner, making no effort to hide his enthusiasm at the prospect of having Sebold accept a passport to treason.

"'How do you know that, Doctor?'

"'We looked into you very thoroughly before you ever left the United States,' said Gassner. 'We are fully aware of your capabilities. You have, for one thing, an excellent mechanical mind, and one given to just the detail that we want in the man that we need to take over the work we have in mind for you.'

"'How in the world did you ever find out so much about me without my knowing it?' asked Sebold, genuinely surprised.

"Gassner said that the Gestapo had an agent right in the Consolidated Aircraft plant, where Sebold had worked as a draftsman, and that this man had supplied all the background data the Himmler organization needed. 'So we know,' said Doctor Gassner, 'that among other things you are a man who is always guided by reason rather than by your feelings. That is why we also know that we could trust you, for you are quite fond of life and just as fond of your family, even though you have had mild disagreements with them—particularly with one of your brothers—since your arrival here in Mulheim-on-Ruhr.'"[7]

Sebold was stunned at the last remark about his brother—he'd been followed the entire time he'd been in Germany. Now in fear for his life and realizing that resisting this threat could place his family in danger, Sebold eventually yielded, agreeing to work with the Gestapo. It seemed he had no other choice. At another meeting he met again with Dr. Gassner as well as another individual who called himself Dr. Renken. He later learned that Renken was actually Major Nickolaus Ritter, the Abwehr's chief of military espionage. They insisted that Sebold make himself available for training at the Hamburg Spy School, where he was to be trained in the use of shortwave radio, Morse code, and microphotography, including how to take photographs using miniature cameras, develop the film, and enlarge the image when a microfilm was received from Germany. Sebold was soon fully immersed in the Abwehr/Gestapo against his will, but with no other recourse while on German soil.

Fortunately, an opportunity presented itself for Sebold to get outside help. His United States passport had been stolen (likely by Gassner to keep him in Germany), and so he needed to go to an American consulate to request a replacement. The nearest was in Cologne, Germany. Once inside the consulate, Sebold requested an urgent meeting with an attaché, who took detailed notes of Sebold's claim of being blackmailed into cooperating with the Nazis, as well as his offer to help the United States instead. Since it would take time to process his request for a new passport, Sebold returned to his mother's home until being summoned back to the consulate.

On his return, he was told that he had been investigated at the highest levels of government and that the United States would very much like him to accept the Nazis' proposition, but that he would be assigned FBI agents in the United States to assist him in acting as a counterspy (later called a double agent). What Sebold did not know is that his offer had been reviewed by Secretary of State Cordell Hull; J. Edgar Hoover, the director of the FBI; and even discussed with President Franklin D. Roosevelt. All were excited to think that they could infiltrate Nazi spy rings operating in the United States while also having a way to send false intelligence back to the Nazis. Sebold's role as Germany's microphotographer and radio operator placed him directly at the center of communication between the German spy network in the United States and Berlin. William Sebold was right in the middle of the conflict between two powerful governments whose opposition to each other was growing by the day.

After Sebold completed his training at the Hamburg spy school, Dr. Gassner accompanied him by train to Genoa, Italy, where

Sebold boarded the SS *Washington* for passage to New York for an arrival on February 8, 1940. This was four months after the declaration of war by France and England against Germany, so it was unsafe for him to depart from a German port. Sebold carried with him four identical microfilms that he was to deliver to four people in the United States—agents of the Nazis who would become part of Sebold's network—as well as a large sum of American cash that would pay these operatives and finance the ambitious plans the Nazis had for Sebold in New York City. The items listed on the microfilm (which was intercepted by the FBI on Sebold's arrival in New York and translated prior to delivering them to the intended recipients) provided a broad picture of what the Nazis hoped to accomplish in America. It is chilling to read:

"1. Find out if International Telegraph and Telephone have offered the French and English governments a new procedure of bombing which works as follows: The airplane is directed by some sort of a ray against the target and crosses a second ray shortly before reaching the target by which the bombs will be released. Try to get hold of all particulars pertaining to the construction of the device, and find out how it has worked in tests and whether there have been negotiations in the French and English governments with the view of selling it to them.

"2. There is said to be a branch factory of the French plant of Potez at Montreal. Find out the exact location, type of aircraft manufactured . . . are they building fighters? . . . how many are they turning out a week? How many employees?

"3. Find out all you can about Professor ——— . . . , an expert for chemical warfare. . . . He is supposed to have developed a new means of protection against mustard gas . . . by which cloth uniforms are impregnated. . . . What is the chemical make-up of the new protection? . . . Is it still being tested by the Army or have orders for it already gone to the chemical industry? If so, to what firms and to what extent?

"4. Find out everything possible about new developments in the line of anti-aircraft guns. We want to know the weight of the gun in firing position, . . . caliber, weight of shell, weight of cartridge, muzzle velocity, highest elevation, range vertically and horizontally, firing speed, fire control. Manufactured by whom, and how many? Delivery dates? Give particulars about gun manufacturing firms, name and location, how many employees, work capacity.

"5. Is there anywhere in the United States an anti-aircraft shell with so-called Electric Eye being manufactured? If so, find out everything you can about experiences gained in tests . . . how are not-exploded shells rendered harmless before reaching the earth? How many meters or feet must the projectile be distant from the airplane in order to be exploded by action of the reflected ray?

"6. Get a copy of United States Senator Barbour's Espionage Law.

"7. Keep us up-to-date in all developments in the aircraft industry. Always keep an eye on all that is going on at the leading plants, especially Curtiss, North American Aircraft, Glenn Martin, Douglass, Boeing, United Aircraft, Lockheed and the leading motor plants, especially Wright and Pratt and Whitney.

"8. The Bell Corporation is said to have developed a cable of high frequency service. . . . Find out if it has been introduced into the American Army, in what frequency range it is used, structure of cable, diameter, covering and capacity of conduction. In what lengths is it being used, surface or underground? What do the plugs look like? Is there any special equipment for laying the cable? Get hold of a sample.

"9. What is new about anti-fog devices?

"10. What is new about bacteriological warfare from airplanes? All details.

"11. Find out all about new gas mask developments and give details.

"12. Pertaining to Sperry Range Finders, find out if latest range finder is equipped to register changes in altitude and how it is being done.

"13. Find out if there are going to Europe whole units or single aircraft with personnel of the US Army and Navy as camouflaged Volunteer Corps. Report immediately when there are any signs of mobilization like calling up volunteers, reestablishment of Drafting Offices and calling in of reserve officers and reservists on a large scale, shipment or take-off of USA units and shipping of large amounts of war materials out of US Army and Navy stores to Europe. State name of steamer and date of departure. Use code for cable reports."[8]

This list reveals that Germany had five major objectives for their United States spy network: (1) steal as many military secrets as possible to save on development time and have the best possible military weapons available; (2) determine if America, which at the time was neutral, was secretly supplying and supporting the French and British; (3) determine if America was secretly preparing to enter the war against Germany; (4) keep track of American industrial capacity in case it was brought to bear against Germany; (5) provide intelligence about shipments from America to Britain so U-boats could attack and destroy the ships and cargo.

What this specific list did not outline but that would become clear in later communications between Sebold and his German contacts is that they also wanted to increase their capacity to initiate sabotage against American government, military, and defense companies as the war progressed.

When Sebold arrived in New York harbor using the Nazi-assigned name of "Harry Sawyer," he was met by agents of the FBI, who brought him up to speed on how they would coordinate with him in his role as a counterspy. It required great finesse for him to communicate with American agents while also interacting with local German operatives in such a way that the Germans did not become suspicious. Sebold managed these competing relationships very well, although it caused him a great deal of stress that occasionally interfered with his health.

To assist Sebold, an FBI agent by the name of James Ellsworth was assigned as a permanent point of contact. Ellsworth had been a missionary for The Church of Jesus Christ of Latter-Day Saints in Germany after World War I and so spoke fluent German. He had a strong work ethic and sense of integrity that matched Sebold's. They quickly became friends, which was fortunate given that Ellsworth would spend nearly two years away from his wife and children while working full-time with Sebold on behalf of the FBI.

Safely back in America with his wife, Bill Sebold quickly became America's most important spy against the interests of his homeland and the Nazi party that had taken the reins of power there.

SETTING UP SHOP IN AMERICA

It takes people and infrastructure to run a spy network. If Sebold was going to insinuate himself into existing networks, he had to gain trust and provide services that made him indispensable. Fortunately for Sebold, he had both German and American money to help with all this, as well as logistical support from the FBI. Dozens of agents would be assigned to follow and document what the German operatives who interacted with William Sebold were doing.

With respect to the people involved, the first step was to introduce himself to the four people Dr. Gassner wanted to receive the microfilms: Frederick Joubert Duquesne, Herman Lang, Everett Minster Roeder, and Lilly Stein.

"Fritz" Duquesne was the leader of this group, an extravagant fellow from South Africa who had a deep-seated hatred of the British. He was a braggart who claimed to have sabotaged the ship on which Lord Horatio Herbert Kitchener, England's Secretary of State for War during World War I, was killed in 1916. Kitchener had been the British Chief of Staff and then Commander in Chief in South Africa's Second Boer War, which is why Duquesne hated him. It is doubtful that Duquesne had anything to do with the sinking, but he bragged about it along with many other exploits he supposedly carried out during the First World War and in subsequent years.

A tall, good-looking man, Duquesne moved easily among the upper crust of both British and American society, but always acted secretly for Germany. The British intelligence service called him the most dangerous man ever to set foot in England. In the years between the wars he played the roles of a newspaper correspondent, magazine writer, lecturer, botanist, and scientist. At the time Sebold met him he was acting as a consultant for "Air Terminal Associates" in a skyscraper in Manhattan. That innocuous title allowed him to gain access to many American companies and factories.

Duquesne was skeptical of Sebold, and, although he used Sebold in the coming years to make microfilms and transmit messages, he always maintained alternate ways of connecting directly with the Abwehr and Gestapo. Even though he was given to exaggeration, Duquesne was still a highly effective spy with many connections and, as the drama unfolded, he proved himself capable of acts of violence and even murder when acting in behalf of Germany. He was always a threat to William Sebold.

Herman Lang was a foreman at the Norden bombsight plant in Brooklyn who had already betrayed America by memorizing and sharing with the Germans many of the key components of what was then America's most closely guarded secret, the Norden bombsight. The Norden was an engineering marvel that used gyroscopes and direct connections to the flight mechanisms of a heavy bomber to provide precision daylight bombing when a target was in view. But without a working model, it was difficult for German engineers to do much with the intelligence Lang had provided them on an earlier visit to Berlin. Plus, in the early days of World War II, the Germans decided to focus on dive bombers rather than heavy bombers, so they never fully exploited the information Lang had given them. As a naturalized German-born resident of New York, Lang had committed treason against the United States by sharing this classified information. At the time he met Sebold, Lang's hope was to secretly steal a working model of the Norden bombsight from the plant and eventually take it to Europe. What he did not know is that the FBI was already aware of his betrayal and had agents in the plant to make sure he could never bring anything out. Lang was a self-centered man who constantly demanded more money from his German hosts and threatened to withdraw from the spy group when they hesitated.

Everett Minster Roeder worked at the Sperry Gyroscope Company. The Sperry gyroscopic rangefinder was of a simpler design than the Norden, and in many ways more useful since it was used on a wider variety of aircraft. Roeder was not known to the FBI prior to Gassner introducing him to Sebold. In the months that followed, Roeder would provide useful industrial espionage to the Germans—except for the fact that with Sebold as an intermediary, the FBI was able to modify critical intelligence to make it useless to the Abwehr. The trick was to allow enough valid information to pass through that the Germans did not become suspicious.

Lilly Stein was a woman who used her beauty and charm to pry secrets out of lonely men working in the war industries. For example, she had a relationship with Edward Karl Heine, an executive at Ford Motor Company, who arranged a tour for her of a Ford aircraft production factory. He also provided detailed written information about Ford's production and capacity. When Stein first met Sebold, she said, "We are doing great things, Mister Sawyer. I know of practically every new development in the Detroit factories. I hope you will find it possible to send good reports about my work as time goes on." She then used a magnifying glass to look at the microfilm Sebold had given her and added, "I already know the answers to some of these questions."[9] She promised to have more information the next time they met.

Dozens of other players would join Sebold in the coming months as he successfully built out his network, but these four were the beginning.

When it came to infrastructure, there were three things Sebold needed to accomplish.

First, he needed to rent office space where he could meet with people. The FBI helped him find an office on the sixth floor of the Newsweek Building on Times Square. They outfitted a plain-looking business office for Sebold. The sign on the door read "Diesel Research Associates," a name that made it reasonable for a diverse cast of characters to show up regularly without raising suspicion. Sebold paid for this office with money received from Germany. But the FBI rented an adjoining room, which they outfitted with state-of-the-art movie cameras and audio equipment. A camouflaged opening in the wall allowed a movie camera to record the meetings Sebold held with his German operatives. Hidden microphones allowed the FBI to listen in on these conversations in real time, both to act on the intelligence gained and to build a case against these people for future use in court proceedings.

Second, Sebold needed to set up a powerful shortwave radio to establish direct communication with Berlin. Two FBI agents were assigned to help Sebold acquire the equipment and to set it up in a remote cottage on Long Island. The house was selected because it allowed FBI agents to gain access without German agents noticing. Dr. Gassner in Berlin had warned Sebold that he would be under surveillance to make sure he didn't double-cross the Gestapo and

Abwehr. Sebold could enter by the front door, while the FBI agents who created the transmissions entered secretly.

After the installation was complete, Sebold took Fritz Duquesne out to see it, and he was impressed. Duquesne sent his first message to Hamburg using a code that had been provided to Sebold, but had to wait a few days until they responded. In the next two years Sebold and his FBI accomplices sent more than 300 messages to Hamburg and received approximately 200.

Third, Sebold needed to outfit a high-quality photo lab to photograph important documents and develop the negatives into microfilm that could easily be carried out of the country by couriers sympathetic to Germany. Many couriers were employees of steamship companies that traveled between the United States and Spain in the early days of the war in Europe.

Although Sebold was new to the scene, he was the assigned paymaster for most of the Germans operating in the New York area, which helped him gain their trust more quickly. It was not long before Sebold, using his assigned name of Harry Sawyer, had established relationships throughout the New York metropolitan area, and he quickly became instrumental in passing the intelligence gained by his operatives along to Germany.

METHODS AND DILEMMAS

Prior to 1940 the US government had almost no resources devoted to safeguarding America's industrial and military secrets. That began to change when President Franklin D. Roosevelt quietly expanded the FBI's authority to surveil suspected foreign agents. It was a complex undertaking, given that many of America's legal and privacy safeguards extended to American-born or naturalized citizens. The FBI had to act with discretion to carefully build a file against people suspected of acting against the United States.

Fortunately, they were able to enlist the help of others. For example, the Duquesne and Ludwig spy rings often sent paper letters through the US mail system to a neutral country like Spain. The FBI was prevented by law from opening these letters, even when they were suspected of containing incriminating information. What the FBI *could* do was to have letters to Spain routed through Bermuda, where British law allowed censors to open and examine the letters. Almost always the written information on the front of a page was harmless. But on the reverse side the Germans would use invisible ink to send sensitive information that violated US laws. The British exposed these letters to heat, which caused the invisible ink to become visible, but not in a way that the ultimate recipient would know that they had been tampered with.

Two other ways that Sebold and his agents sent information was by shortwave radio and microfilm. The Nazi spies had to be careful in their use of the shortwave radio since it was easy for American agents to detect that broadcasts were occurring. One of the first messages Duquesne gave to Sebold to transmit to Berlin by shortwave radio read as follows:

"Rolls Royce have engine designed to go into the wings like a meat sandwich. Lycoming have one also. I sent blueprints by China. Allies ordered 10,000 additional machine guns, motorcycles, and sidecars. US Intelligence getting news through Myron Taylor in Vatican. A priest there is bringing it to him. The SS *Champlain* is taking munitions cargo from the USA in a day or so. She is armed with anti-submarine and anti-aircraft protection. She may carry members of the French Purchasing Commission. She is going to be picked up by a convoy off Bermuda. She is going to Cherbourg."[10]

The information about the SS *Champlain* put many lives at risk, since U-boats would be dispatched to intercept and sink the ship. But what should the FBI do with the information? If they failed to transmit it exactly as Duquesne dictated it to Sebold, there was a risk that Duquesne would send the same information via other means to see if Sebold was manipulating his messages, a common counterintelligence tactic.

The FBI instructed Sebold to send the message exactly as written, but they warned the SS *Champlain* to make minor adjustments to its sailing time and course to increase its chances of survival, just one of hundreds of decisions that had to be made about protecting the integrity of the operation while not endangering innocent lives unnecessarily. The problem was that each interaction with Duquesne and his network let the FBI know that there were other as yet unknown operatives out there. By keeping the network active they could cast a wider net.

While Sebold was never brought into a discussion of how accurate the information was his informers were bringing him, the FBI was astonished at how voluminous and how precise many of the transmissions were. For example, another operative by the name of Frederick Ludwig sent this message in invisible ink that was decoded in the Bermuda laboratory:

> Re: Bell Aircraft Corp.—Buffalo—
> Employment: Oct. 15, 1939—1,064
> Jan. 1, 1940—1,160
> Oct. 15, 1940—3,237
> Dec. 31, 1940—4,300
> Backlog:
> Oct. 15, 1940, about $65 [million]
> Jan 1941, about $60 [million]
> Production: Oct 1940:
> About 3 P-39 for US Army and
> 3 P-40 for Britain
> . . . The SS *Egyptian Prince*, 3,490 tons was seen on Apr 20 and 22nd at Pier 96—black hull—buff superstructure—On April 20 on barges near Pier 90 were 4 bombers (Hudsons) and three mosquito boats—on April 18 at Pier 4—Brooklyn—45 St—the British freighter

Welsh Prince—dark gray hull—yellow superstructure—
black funnel—at Pier 3 a Dutch freighter—at Pier 2 an
English steamer of about six thousand tons—black hull—
buff superstructure—black funnel—sorry could not get
name.[11]

All the information in this message was both accurate and
timely—and of great interest to war planners in Berlin and U-boat
captains in the Atlantic. How had Ludwig gained such detailed and
specific information?

GERMAN SPY NETWORKS IN THE UNITED STATES

In the crucial years leading up to America's becoming a belliger-
ent in the war, there were five primary German spy rings operating
in America. Sebold insinuated himself into three of these networks
and indirectly helped the FBI identify the other two.

The Fritz Duquesne Spy Ring, the most prominent players of
which were involved primarily in industrial espionage, was particularly adept at stealing American military aircraft design and bombing
mechanism secrets. Herman Lang and Everett Minster Roeder spied
on the Norden and Sperry bombsight manufacturers. Lilly Stein and
Edward Heine spied on Ford and other war contractors. Leo Waalen
provided detailed information on the Higgins Motor Torpedo boats
produced in Louisiana. Also instrumental in the group's activities
were Wilhelm Siegler and Franz Stigler, who served as couriers while
working as cooks and waiters on the SS *America*. Duquesne had
personally infiltrated many war production factories up and down
the East Coast, which he used to provide production statistics to
Germany so they could estimate US capacity.

The Axel Wheeler-Hill Spy Ring was fronted by Axel
Wheeler-Hill, who worked as a delivery driver for a soft drink
company, a cover to drive right up to industrial locations or the
Brooklyn and New York piers without suspicion. He'd strike up

conversations with workers while unloading soda, in the process learning a great deal about the activities and output of their employers. His associate Felix Jahnke used a similar technique in the taverns near the docks to get inebriated dockworkers to talk freely about shipping manifests, ship departure dates, and even hidden armaments on board the ships. This information was useful to U-boats prowling the North Atlantic for targets of destruction. Axel Wheeler-Hill also recruited a thirty-seven-year-old mechanic at Bendix Air named Carl Alfred Reupert to sneak out aircraft blueprints at night, which would be photographed and sent to Germany by microfilm. What Wheeler-Hill did not know is that Reupert secretly reported the recruitment to the FBI. The FBI in turn fed Reupert bogus diagrams that hindered rather than advanced German aircraft design.

The Frederick Ludwig Group was one of the most successful groups in America, providing intelligence to both German and Japanese spy agencies. Early in the life of the group, a German operative, Ludwig von der Osten (living undercover as an Argentinian working with the Spanish consulate named Julio Lopez), was assassinated by being struck by a car in Times Square. After his death, the New York City police searched his apartment and found detailed maps of military installations along the East Coast. More chilling, they found a highly specific map of Pearl Harbor, Hawaii, showing where US battleships and aircraft carriers were assigned. This was in March 1941, ten months prior to the Japanese aerial attack on December 7.

As the FBI began to untangle von der Osten's relationships, they found that he worked with another German agent by the name of Frederick Ludwig who occasionally used William Sebold to send wireless messages to Germany. Ludwig was a very self-disciplined operator who specialized in highly technical espionage. With his accomplices—Lucy Boehlmer, a skilled stenographer and typist, and

Dr. Paul Borchardt, a highly trained military analyst—he purchased American technical magazines that Borchardt examined for useful information. They also recruited agents in American production facilities, and even had a member of their group, Rene Froelich, who was serving in the US Army at a base in Georgia. Froelich was able to send messages about the number of troops in training and the specialties that were offered, as well as steal copies of training manuals and technical specifications that Borchardt used to write summaries for the benefit of the Abwehr in Berlin.

Ludwig used every method available to communicate with Germany. He often used Sebold to send his urgent messages by shortwave, but he also had access to his own shortwave radio (which the FBI hunted down so they could disable it at a moment's notice if needed). He sent some reports using invisible ink through the US Mail by way of Bermuda, which gave the British censors the chance to intercept the messages. And he was prolific in his use of microfilm taken and developed by Sebold.

In midsummer 1941, Ludwig and Lucy Boehlmer took an extended car trip down the East Coast, stopping at nearly every military base or war production facility along the way. Because the FBI was aware of their status, they were discretely trailed the entire length of the trip, and the FBI took photos of Ludwig and Boehlmer taking photos of top-secret facilities. The German agents would frequent bars near factories or army bases after a shift change or at the end of the day. Boehlmer would strike up conversations with the single men at the bar, and it wasn't long before they were talking freely to her. It is astonishing, in hindsight, how casual American workers were with confidential information. On one occasion, however, an astute US Army officer from Camp Meade suspected the Germans and almost blew the FBI's cover.

"Ludwig and Lucy went to a saloon near the camp. Who showed up but the soldier that Lucy had struck up a flirtation with that morning. Lucy and the soldier and Ludwig started to drink beer. A lot of other soldiers began drifting into the saloon. Pretty soon Ludwig was setting up beer for about a dozen of them. Along toward ten o'clock some of the boys began to feel their drinks and became talkative. Ludwig had plenty of questions to ask them. The G-Men [FBI] knew that because they were sitting near by. He asked the soldiers where they were from, details about previous camps they had been in, and many well-thought-out questions about what was going on at Camp Meade.

"The soldiers, not realizing what they were doing, gave the right answers. What grist this was for the Borchardt [analyst] mill!

"Ludwig's watery-blue eyes were glistening behind his glasses, and his pasty face had taken on a flush. He was riding high, wide and handsome.

"The clock wore on. It was almost eleven. A couple of nice-looking soldiers came in—just the type of boys who are going to die for Uncle Sam. These two ordered soft drinks. They were attracted immediately to the group at Ludwig's table. One of the G-Men nudged his partner.

"'There's going to be some fun here, I think,' he said.

"The two newcomers frowned on their talkative buddies. Well they might. The American Army was not in the least represented by this handful of khaki-clad boys who had taken on too many beers and who were talking too much.

"In about twenty minutes, the G-Men noticed that a cold fury was sweeping through the two sober soldiers. They were listening to every word that was going on—every syllable of every artful question that Ludwig was cunningly putting to the free-loaders. Finally, both of the soft-drinkers stood up and walked over to the group at the table.

"'Listen, fellows,' said one of them to the soldiers, 'you better get back to camp. You're being taken for a ride by this German!' The spy looked up timidly. Then he pointed at himself and asked innocently, 'Me? You are talking about me?'

"'Yes, you! I think you're a spy! You've been milking military secrets out of these fellows here after they were nuts enough to let you get them drunk.'

"The soldiers seemed suddenly to sober. A rumble ran through the group. The proprietor came running over, he didn't want any fuss in his place.

"'There won't be any trouble here,' shouted one of the soldiers who had talked to Ludwig. He looked around meaningly at his pals. 'Not in here, huh, fellows?'

"The boys caught on. 'No,' one of them answered, his voice hoarse with anger at being betrayed. 'We won't do it here; let's take the old bastard outside and tear 'im apart.'

"While Ludwig cringed in a corner and Lucy stifled a gasp, the soldiers began to converge slowly on the German spy."[12]

The FBI agents quickly moved to the two sober soldiers and whispered their true identities, asking for their help in defusing the situation. They were not yet done learning where Ludwig and Boehlmer intended to travel, so the two soldiers were able to defuse the situation just long enough for Ludwig and Boehlmer to make their escape. The FBI agents were pleased that at least a couple of soldiers recognized the danger. After this encounter, the German spies continued their journey, eventually turning west and "inspecting" military camps and industrial facilities along the Florida Gulf Coast, Alabama, and then turning north to Tennessee and West Virginia. By the time they returned to New York they had hundreds of pages of notes to turn over to their analyst. He created detailed summaries that were forwarded to Germany, but only after they were intercepted—and in some cases modified—by the FBI.

The Anastase Vonsiatsky (VV) Spy Ring was one group tracked by the FBI that did *not* intersect with William Sebold.

Anastase Vonsiatsky (sometimes known as "VV") was an extremely wealthy White Russian immigrant to the United States who owned a fabulous 200-acre estate in Connecticut. He was the leader of the International Russian Revolutionary Fascist Party. In this role he sent out seemingly outrageous declarations on behalf of his organization, leading some to think he was a screwball. But the FBI knew enough of his underground activities to take him seriously. He created a network to pass intelligence through Mexico to Japan using submarines. Some of this information was then forwarded from Japan to Germany. His associates included a Dr. Willumeit in Chicago; William Kunze in Camden, New Jersey; Wolfgang Ebell, a doctor in El Paso, Texas, who frequently crossed the border into Mexico; and a Protestant minister in Philadelphia, the Reverend Kurt Molzahn. There was also the unnamed Ukrainian minister to whom Fiodore Wozniak applied to be a saboteur, but who was secretly working with the FBI. The group succeeded in passing detailed maps of Hawaii and West Coast military facilities over to Japan.

Carl and Werner von Clemm were brothers but not German spies; they were diamond merchants who used their connections in Nazi-occupied Belgium to help the Germans secretly export high quality Belgian diamonds (forbidden under US law at the time) into the United States where the Nazis planned to sell them to finance their operations in the United States—in particular to fund sabotage operations after the war in Europe began in earnest. This would not only supply the Nazis with a new source of income, it would also disrupt American markets.

The FBI placed great significance on monitoring these German spy networks. In fact, J. Edgar Hoover assigned himself as the lead supervisor on the case—the only open investigation in which he took an active role. The goal was to build a solid case against all operatives in the networks so that when they were arrested, a jury would find them guilty. It required patience to watch their malicious activities without acting too soon—before all the players were identified and an adequate case was built against them.

SEBOLD BECOMES ANXIOUS
–HIS HEALTH DETERIORATES

Sebold was remarkably cool when dealing with his German contacts. For example, sixteen months into the investigation he had an ominous encounter with Duquesne.

"[The] next day, Fritz Duquesne, the spy master, dropped into [Sebold's office] in the Newsweek Building. G-Men in an adjoining room, which was wired for sound, heard Fritz complaining about a quarrel he had had with his mistress, the socialite who was living with him in a sumptuous apartment in the Seventies, off Central Park West. The girl had begun to suspect that an old failing of Fritz's, namely, susceptibility to the opposite sex had taken hold of him again.

"'We'd be in a terrible mess, Fritz,' said Sebold, 'if that girl ever turned on you and talked to the FBI.'

"Duquesne's smoky blue eyes narrowed, and he fell into thoughtful silence. Then he looked up at Sebold, his eyes mere slits now, and his voice took on an ominous rumbling quality as he said, 'We'd be in more of a mess if *you* went to the FBI.'

"'I don't know what you mean, Fritz,' said Sebold, who hoped that he was successfully shielding his alarm and at the same time feigning surprise.

"'I mean just this,' said the Boer. 'If I ever found out that you weren't on the level, I'd kill you with my own hands.'

"'But I *am* on the level!' protested Sebold, who was now introducing a note of anger because the FBI had told him that that was the thing to do if he wanted to appear falsely accused. Duquesne ignored Sebold and went on with his own train of thought. 'That would make five dead right in your family,' he said, 'you, your mother, two brothers and a sister.'

"Sebold asked Duquesne why he had ever come to doubt his integrity. Fritz was silent for a while, and then he laughed. 'Forget what I said, Harry,'—he always referred to Sebold as Harry Sawyer, the name assigned by the Gestapo—'and let's go out and have a drink. I'm just jumpy, that's all. I'd damned near suspect myself at times.'

"'What are you jumpy about, Fritz?' asked Sebold, with simulated solicitation.

"'Those FBI bastards. That man Hoover's into everything.' Fritz nodded his head toward the wall between Sebold's front and the room occupied by the agents. 'For all I know,' he said, 'some of them might be in there.'

"Sebold pretended to be alarmed. 'You could be right, Fritz,' he said. 'Tell you what; let's go in there now and find out what's going on.'

"Sebold made it a point to stall just long enough for the agents in the next room to hide their equipment. Then he and Duquesne went out into the hallway and knocked on the door of the office occupied by the G-Men. Precisely what happened then cannot be disclosed here. Suffice it to say that the G-Men had prepared well in advance for such an eventuality as this, and Duquesne found himself in a front [legitimate business] that looked even more genuine than Sebold's.

"Over drinks later, Duquesne began to laugh at how jittery he had been."[13]

Sebold had dodged a bullet that could have ruined the entire investigation, but he stayed cool and carried it off. Later, FBI assistant director Percy Foxworth said to Sebold, "Bill, you are a great patriot; you are risking your life, and the lives of four of your blood relatives for your adopted country." Sebold replied simply, "That's all right, Mr. Foxworth."[14]

But it did take a toll on Sebold. Since incurring injuries and maladies from World War I his physical health had been perilous. It also affected his emotional stability. So while Sebold maintained a steady voice and calm demeanor with the Germans, he sometimes needed emotional support from Jim Ellsworth and others in the FBI to cope. At one point his distress became so severe that Sebold reported that he could not eat or sleep. An appointment was scheduled with Dr. Philip Goodhardt, an expert in nervous conditions. In his report back to the FBI, Goodhardt reported that Sebold said he had lost more than forty pounds in the previous two years, that he worried frequently, and that just two years earlier he'd had stomach surgery for ulcers. In Sebold's version of his visit to Dr. Goodhardt he said that the doctor told him that his was a case "of considerable nervous strain, that he was in a very rundown condition, and under severe shock and strain." Ellsworth later reported that "we sent him to a nerve specialist who attested that he was on the verge of a nervous breakdown, prescribed rest, and plenty of good food."[15]

Loyalty was paramount to William Sebold, both his loyalty to the United States and the expected loyalty of those who were supporting him in his counterspy efforts. The greatest risk to the Sebold operation would be if he came to believe the FBI did not trust him or appreciate him. Fortunately, Jim Ellsworth was a steady hand who stood by Sebold as a faithful friend. The FBI did all they could to help Sebold since having such a well-placed collaborator within the Nazi spy rings was invaluable to the investigation. But after nearly two years the investigation was approaching the point that action needed to be taken to protect the USA from the Nazi spies—and to protect William Sebold from being discovered.

THE FBI CLOSES IN

In late June 1941, the situation was becoming perilous. So deeply had the various spy rings burrowed themselves into America's war infrastructure that they were about to transmit the most damaging top-secret intelligence in American history. The FBI had also picked up increasing evidence that many were getting ready to sneak out of the country by steamship to neutral ports. J. Edgar Hoover made the decision to bring them in. Arrest warrants were issued, and the FBI made its move. There were no shootouts, or standoffs; it was really rather quiet.

Thirty-three members of the Duquesne and Wheeler-Hill networks were arrested one by one with little incident. Duquesne was arrested by an agent who had been living in an apartment next to his for several years—Duquesne had no idea he'd been under surveillance in his own home.

The initial charge was conspiracy to violate the espionage laws. At this point none of them knew that Sebold was the person who'd turned them in. That would be revealed during their trial in December.

When Kurt Ludwig learned of the arrests of the Duquesne agents, he was angry. This was known to the FBI because he sent a letter to the Gestapo in Berlin that was intercepted by the British in Bermuda. In the letter he suggested that those who were arrested were incompetent and lazy, but that they posed a danger to him and all other operatives still in the United States if they started talking. He made the chilling request that word be sent to them through their attorneys that if they did not remain quiet, their families back in Germany would be arrested and executed. Tough talk, but time was running out.

Ludwig decided to leave the country. Fearing that he was being followed by the FBI on the East Coast, he started a cross-country trip through the northern states. He did have chutzpah—even while preparing to leave, he stopped at defense plants along the route to take more photos. In Butte, Montana, he burned some documents in a rented cabin, then shipped two suitcases back to New Jersey. The FBI recovered the burned remnants of the highly classified documents, enough to show that Ludwig should not be allowed to escape to Japan as a transit point to Germany. He was arrested quietly in a small town in Washington State in late July. His audacity continued when he offered to bribe his jailer, special deputy marshal Ray Killian, with $50,000 if he'd let him escape. Killian played along for a while but made sure that "attempting to bribe a federal officer" was added to the list of charges against Ludwig. The other members of his group, including Lucy Boehlmer and Dr. Paul Borchardt, were picked up the following day.

Anastase Vonsiatsky and his group were successful in transferring a suitcase full of classified documents to a Japanese submarine off the coast of Mexico. They did not know that all the information inside the suitcase was useless, planted by the FBI by giving false information to the VV informants. Vonsiatsky was arrested in Providence, Rhode Island, and three others of his group in Chicago. The fifth member of the group, William Kunze, was arrested by Mexican authorities as Kunze attempted to escape to Japan.

Werner von Clemm, the diamond importer who had smuggled high-quality Belgian diamonds into the United States was arrested for falsifying import documents. The diamonds were confiscated and von Clemm imprisoned.

SEBOLD TESTIFIES—ALL ARE CONVICTED

Of thirty-three operatives arrested on the charge of espionage, nineteen pleaded guilty. The remaining fourteen went on trial on September 3, 1941. The star witness against them was William Sebold, backed up by FBI movies, dictograph recordings, photos, and incriminating documents seized at the time of their arrest. The trial lasted more than two months. On December 13, 1941—just six days after the Japanese attack on Pearl Harbor, the jury delivered guilty verdicts for all fourteen defendants. Duquesne and Herman Lang were both sentenced to eighteen years in prison. The other sentences ranged from fifteen months to eighteen years, with major players receiving at least sixteen years. At the trial, Duquesne expressed but one desire—to strangle William Sebold with his own hands![16]

The Ludwig network went on trial on February 8, 1942, and all were found guilty. Ludwig, Borchardt, and Froelich received sentences of twenty years, with other members of the group receiving fifteen. Lucy Boehlmer turned states' evidence against her coconspirators in exchange for a reduced sentence of five years.

Werner von Clemm was indicted on charges of falsifying import declarations with respect to the Belgian diamonds and was sentenced to two years in a federal penitentiary. At the end of his term he was sent to an internment camp for the balance of the war.

Anastase Vonsiatsky and his five coconspirators were indicted on the charge of "conspiracy to collect and deliver to the German and Japanese governments information relating to the numbers, personnel, disposition, equipment, arms and morale of the Army of the United States; the location, size, capacity and other features of military establishments essential to the national defense of the United States." All were convicted in trials conducted in Hartford, Connecticut. Though not active in their ring, Fiodore Wozniak, the famed World War I saboteur, was arrested in July 1941 along with dozens of other potential saboteurs. Eventually, nearly 11,000 German-born or naturalized citizens were sent to seven internment camps for the duration of the war.

The FBI recorded in its official history, "As a result of the massive investigation, the FBI—and America—entered the war with confidence that there was no major German espionage network hidden in US society."[17]

SEBOLD GOES INTO "WITNESS PROTECTION"

William Sebold had become a hero in the national press. His testimony under severe distress had been damning for both the defendants and for the Nazi regime. Here are some examples of newspaper headlines from the trial:

"'Trapped by the Gestapo during a trip to his native Germany, a naturalized American citizen was forced under threat of death to act as a Nazi spy in America.'

"According to the *Eagle,* the 'Gestapo' employed 'the gangster "or else" threat' . . .

"'Hitler Couldn't Scare Sebold, Spy Trial Star,' the *Boston Globe* said. 'So He Helped FBI Round Up Nazi Agents in USA.' . . .

"On September 9, Sebold continued his narrative up to the point when the Centerport radio station made contact with Hamburg, which dominated the coverage in the next day's papers. The *Times* called the communications link 'probably the greatest hoax perpetrated on the vaunted Nazi military intelligence to date.'

"The *Daily Mirror* said the FBI played 'Nazi espionage heads in Germany for a bunch of suckers.'"[18]

After the prosecution completed its questioning of Sebold, the defense attacked him ruthlessly, at one point asking for the names and addresses of his relatives in Germany. Sebold replied angrily that he did not think he should have to answer that question in open court in front of Nazi collaborators. The judge agreed and chastised the attorney. At one point in the trial one of the defendants shouted out that Sebold was an "SOB traitor." The anger against him was palpable. But Sebold persisted.

After days of testimony that both humiliated and condemned the Gestapo and their agents in the United States, Bill Sebold's life was in danger. Even before the case was given to the jury, Sebold had left New York with his wife, first to Washington, DC, and then to a new life in San Francisco as one of the first people to enter an early version of the witness protection program. It was not an overreaction. In 1942, eight German saboteurs were landed on the East Coast of the United States by German U-boats. Fortunately, the FBI knew they were coming and arrested all of them. After their trials, six went to the electric chair. Two were spared because they cooperated with the FBI. One of the two who lived, George Dasch, later recounted being given a file on Sebold while Dasch was still in Hamburg, in which he was asked by an Abwehr instructor, "What do you think of that [SOB]?" Dasch had responded, "I tell you there is no stone big enough for him to hide under. We will get him."[19]

Once in California, Sebold started a job in the defense industry. But his bad health continued to afflict him, and he had to take time off from work for both nervous conditions and physical maladies. He also became agitated when he learned that several of the people at the factory where he worked had figured out that he was the famous counterspy from New York City. The FBI agreed that it was unsafe for him to return and helped him find another job.

In 1946, Sebold received the good news that his family had been spared in Germany, and that his mother was still alive. He thought of returning to visit her or having her move to California, but his health took another bad turn with a return of his ulcers as well as a broken vertebrae that made it impossible for him to work.

Another torment in his life was that after the war, former Nazis in Germany spoke openly of his betrayal of his homeland in articles and newspapers. This included Herman Lang, who had been sent to East Germany after he lost his American citizenship. These attacks depressed Sebold and he wanted to speak out to defend his honor, but the FBI convinced him that the best response was to simply ignore it and live his life in America in peace.

In the coming years Sebold had some happy times, according to Jim Ellsworth, but he continued to struggle financially, emotionally, and physically. His wife had him committed to a psychiatric hospital in the later years of his life and he died at the Napa State Hospital on February 16, 1970; the cause of death listed on his death certificate read that he "suffered from manic depression."[20]

It was a hard end for a brave and courageous man who lived his life with integrity. His FBI handler, Jim Ellsworth, remained a friend to the end.

"He wrote about Bill Sebold one last time in a postretirement journal, narrating the tale of an immigrant who so honored the democratic ideals of his adopted homeland that he was prepared to stand in its defense. 'He told me that he had found everything in this country wonderful,' Ellsworth recalled. 'He could go from city to city without registering with the police as he had to in Germany. He could follow any occupation that he pleased. He had all the personal liberties that he had missed in Germany. And so when he took the oath of allegiance, he really meant it and made up his mind that if ever he could prove his devotion to the country he would do so.'"[21]

Having presented the FBI with what assistant director D. M. Ladd called "the most outstanding case in the Bureau's history," William Sebold proved his devotion to the United States as no one else could.

CHAPTER 3

MARLENE DIETRICH

HOLLYWOOD ACTOR SPIES ON THE NAZIS

INTRODUCTION

Virtually everyone in America knew Marlene Dietrich in the glamour days of Hollywood. In the 1920s and 1930s she was a German version of Greta Garbo—exotic, foreign-born, and beautiful. Marlene was an actress who rose to the pinnacle of fame because of her astonishingly beautiful face, her sultry contralto singing voice, and her lithe and sensual body. She lived an extravagant lifestyle of almost unimaginable wealth and fame, and yet was always struggling to pay her bills. Pre–World War II photos of Dietrich show her with handsome men, expensive cars, and beautiful gowns and jewels. She was also known for wearing very masculine clothing, including suits with wide lapels and men's hats and shoes. This added to her allure as a German-born but naturalized American citizen who conveyed both strength and vulnerability in the many and varied roles she played on film. Dietrich traveled extensively in Europe, including to her hometown of Berlin, as well as to Paris, Rome, and London.

It would be easy to judge her as nothing more than a shallow, spoiled celebrity who placed her own interests ahead of others. But as the Nazi party gained strength in Germany, Dietrich revealed a deeper, stronger side of herself as she resisted Nazi entreaties to return home to make movies, and even more so in World War II when she worked actively in the USO (United Services Organizations) to boost troop morale at the very front lines of the European war. Director Billy Wilder remarked that by the end of the war Dietrich had spent more time at the front lines than General Eisenhower. She visited field hospitals, performed onstage, ate army food with the enlisted men in their tents on the battlefield, and used her influence and money to help resettle war refugees.

In peacetime, she traveled with seventeen large steamer trunks full of clothes, makeup, and jewels to sustain her glamorous image. On tour with the USO, she made do with fifty-five pounds of luggage, including costumes. Most of the time she was in Army uniform, and often slept in field tents. It was a sharp contrast to the glamour of her civilian life, but she never expressed anything but gratitude for the chance to be on the road in support of the troops.

While this very public support role was well known to most Americans, she played a quieter part initiated by the Office of Strategic Services (OSS), in working actively to demoralize German troops in the field. Who can say how many American GI lives were saved by her efforts?

For these activities in support of the troops, Marlene Dietrich, the girl from Berlin, was the first female recipient of the American Medal of Freedom, the highest award given to civilians who render significant aid to the United States in time of war. She was also named a commander of the *Legion d'Honneur* by France. Even though she was later criticized by some Germans for siding with

America in the war, she never hesitated in standing up for freedom and against what she viewed as a Nazi plague that brought destruction to her homeland.

BORN IN BERLIN—A STAR IN HOLLYWOOD

Marie Magdalene Dietrich was born in the Schoenberg area of Berlin on December 27, 1901. Her mother, Josefine Felsing, came from a wealthy family that owned a clockmaking business, and who were distressed when she married a police lieutenant from a plebian family. Marlene (she chose this name at age eleven by combining her first and middle names) was the younger of two daughters. Several years after her father passed away in 1907, her mother married a young aristocrat, Eduard von Losch, a lieutenant in the Grenadiers. This elevated the family's status. Unfortunately, von Losch died in 1916 from injuries suffered in World War I. His parents wanted nothing to do with Josefine and her daughters, and so the family struggled again. Twice widowed, the Dietriches were on their own.

Josefine ran a highly regimented household that left very little room for pleasure and laughter. It was all about duty and honor. Having suffered a social decline when married to Dietrich, and then spurned by the von Losch family, Josefine was particularly sensitive to avoiding any scandal that could further erode the family's social standing. That was a problem for Marlene. She adored her maternal grandmother, Elisabeth Felsing, a grand dame who indulged Marlene with chocolate and cake and regaled her with stories of glamour and fine living. Her grandmother was almost the exact opposite of her humorless daughter, and Marlene aspired to be like Elisabeth.

In the desperate years of World War I, in which the risk of starvation was an ever-present reality, Marlene found refuge in the movies. She loved the glamorous female stars and handsome leading men. After the war, she flirted with young men and aspired to be an actress, both of which she kept secret from her mother, since

Josefine considered actors to be on the very lowest rung of society. She loved every type of dance, including the provocative ones that became popular in the postwar era. Eventually, Josefine sent her wayward daughter off to boarding school at Weimar to improve her skills as a violinist and to get her away from her theater friends. Marlene found the school stuffy and confining, but adapted to the military style of daily drills, having spent her life in such a regimented home. She practiced the violin relentlessly—so much so that she developed tendinitis, which ended her mother's dreams of her career in an orchestra.

Returning to Berlin, but unwilling to submit to her mother's direction, she set out to become an actress. She loved the stage and landed parts in the chorus of a number of professional theaters. She married in 1923 and bore her only child, Maria Sieber, in 1924. She continued to do well on stage and started to get substantial roles in European film. Some critics considered her Germany's equivalent of the Swedish-born Greta Garbo. However, Marlene had no recognition in America, the center of moviemaking. Still, she worked diligently at her craft and made good money to support the family, since her husband seldom held a job. She did not use her money to build financial security; her daughter, Maria, remembers that her mother spent all of it.

"As a very young child, I saw luxuries come and go, be replaced by more luxuries, without any fanfare or particular excitement. No 'Look everyone—I got it! The coat I have been saving for, the one I wanted for so long . . . It's mine! Isn't it wonderful? Let's celebrate!' My mother just appeared one day with a mink coat, threw it on a chair, from where it slipped to the floor, lying there forgotten while she strode off to the kitchen to cook dinner."[1]

By this point in her marriage Marlene and her husband, Rudi Sieber, had little romantic interest in each other, but it suited

Marlene to be married to the father of her daughter. She continued to support the family, a pattern that endured throughout her life.

Marlene's big break came in 1929 when she was cast in the leading role of Lola Lola in the German movie *Blue Angel.* She played a cabaret singer. The film was a popular and financial success. Directed by Josef von Sternberg, an extremely successful American director, he persuaded Paramount Pictures to offer Marlene a series of roles in Hollywood. Leaving her family in Berlin, she moved to Hollywood, where she acted in a series of well-received movies, including *Morocco,* for which she received an Academy Award nomination. After the success of *Morocco,* Paramount offered her $250,000 to star in two movies per year, the equivalent of $4.8 million in 2021-adjusted dollars. Marlene Dietrich had become a star. At the height of her career, she earned a remarkable $450,000 per film.

Yet her life wasn't easy. She was a diligent worker who was never late to a film shoot, and who did whatever it took to get a scene just right. On one occasion, director von Sternberg required her to pull on a heavy rope eight times to simulate the ringing of a church bell. Suspended from the rope was a large metal crucifix that slammed into her legs every time she pulled the rope. Marlene had to repeat this scene fifty times before von Sternberg was satisfied. Dietrich never complained, even though it bloodied and bruised her legs. She walked with a limp for many days afterward.

In addition to her acting success, many of the songs she sang in the movies became popular recordings. In between pictures she went home to Berlin to visit her family, and while there recorded a bestselling album of German songs.

In 1937, her career stalled because a few of her films did poorly at the box office. While in London, officials of the Nazi Party approached her to return to Germany to make pictures, promising her lucrative contracts and fame as the leading lady of the Third Reich cinema. This is what she had dreamed of as a child, yet she not only refused their offer, she returned to the United States and applied for US citizenship. She wanted nothing to do with the Nazis.

In 1939, just before the outbreak of war, she accepted a leading role in a Joe Pasternak-directed western, *Destry Rides Again*, starring opposite Jimmy Stewart. In spite of the fantastic money she had made in the previous decade, she was broke and needed the money. Playing the part of a barroom dancer, Frenchie, she put her whole heart and soul into the role, even insisting on doing her own fight scene where she and another woman scratch and brawl on the floor. In the end, the good-hearted Frenchie warns Stewart's character that he's about to be ambushed. In doing so, she is killed in the crossfire—a heroine sacrificing for the hero. The movie was a great success and revived her career.

Then the war came, and everything changed for Marlene Dietrich.

DIETRICH SUPPORTS AMERICA IN WORLD WAR II SELLING WAR BONDS

As a naturalized American citizen, Marlene Dietrich felt and behaved like an American. Yet, as a native-born German, she felt that she somehow shared in the responsibility for this new war that Germany had declared. At least she felt responsible to try to bring it to an early end. So, in 1942 and 1943, she traveled back and forth across the United States to promote the sale of war bonds to help finance the war. She stood on street corners, went to factories, made pitches in cafes, and sang in nightclubs in an attempt to use her celebrity to sell the bonds. For her indefatigable efforts, she is credited with raising more than a million dollars to sustain the war effort.

There was a poignant side to all this, as she pointed out:

"I go on tour to collect money for the bombs that fall on Berlin. That's where my mother lives, and I haven't heard from her since the beginning of the war."[2]

Like so many others who had relatives on the other side of the war, Dietrich endured the misery of not knowing her family's fate. Fortunately, her daughter, Maria, had moved to America and was old enough to get married to an American, Dean Goodman, a struggling comedian. Maria was in acting school, so it fell to Marlene to support them as well as her husband, Rudi. In spite of all her success, she was still broke.

THE HOLLYWOOD CANTEEN, PATRIOTIC FILMS, AND RADIO BROADCASTS

Another way Hollywood supported the war effort was by opening the Hollywood Canteen, a restaurant and dance hall for service members about to depart to the South Pacific. Food and drinks were free and often the world's most famous stars were cooking and serving. Marlene Dietrich was happy to join in this small effort to cheer up the lives of men about to go to battle. She had a domestic side—usually cooking her own meals at home for whatever friends or family came by—and now she cooked hamburgers as a demonstration of her good will and patriotism.

She also made a patriotic propaganda film, *Pittsburgh*, that urged Americans on the home front to put aside domestic quarrels in order to support the troops abroad.

Marlene visited Army hospitals, where she sang and met with injured troops to cheer them up. She also made radio broadcasts appealing to people's patriotism, which led to even more sales of war bonds to people who listened to one of their favorite screen stars. Perhaps her German birth added to her impact—a native German actively fighting for America.

THE UNITED SERVICES ORGANIZATION

Though busy helping the Allied war effort, it was not enough for Marlene to remain passively in America, far away from danger. She volunteered for the USO and received her commission as a captain on June 29, 1943. This was not an honorary title; her USO identification card read: "In event of capture by the enemy [the bearer] is entitled to be treated as a prisoner of war, and . . . s/he will be given the treatment and afforded privileges as an officer in the Army of the United States with the grade of captain."[3]

While her life was about to take an austere turn, she still had style. For example, her tailor-made USO uniform came from Saks Fifth Avenue. The famed comedian Danny Thomas was the emcee of her show, and he took Marlene under his wing to teach her the ropes of surviving in the military and how to handle the crowds of young soldiers. Her first trip with the USO was to Algiers in North Africa, where she sang her first concert. She joked with Danny Thomas, danced, and sang some of her trademark songs. Most famous was "Lili Marlene," originally a German song written by a lonely soldier in World War I who wanted to come home to his girlfriend. So popular was her singing of this nostalgic tune that people dubbed it "The Soldiers' Song of World War II,"[4] actually comforting enlisted men on both sides of the fight. Other songs of hers also became famous, and were part of her program wherever she traveled, including "The Boys in the Backroom" (from the movie *Destry Rides Again*), "You Do Something to Me," and "Taking a Chance on Love." She also played music on a handsaw, a skill she learned in her cabaret days before her film career took off. Her concerts were always a great hit with the soldiers and their officers, who appreciated this boost to morale at just the right time.

Here is a description of how she and Danny worked together to excite the crowd:

> "Fellahs! I've got bad news! We were expecting Marlene Dietrich—but she went out for dinner with a general and she hasn't shown up . . ." This planned "tease" got the anticipated groans, the boos. Suddenly, from the

back of the theater, the unmistakable voice called: "No! No! I'm here! . . . I'm here!" In uniform, carrying a small suitcase, she appeared, running down the aisle toward the stage. By the time she reached the microphone, she had pulled off her tie and was beginning to unbutton her khaki shirt. "I'm not with any general—I'm here! I've just got to change into . . ." She was down to the last button and the GIs howled. She "suddenly" remembered that she was not alone. "Ooh! Sorry, boys, I'll just be a second," and disappeared into the wings. Danny called after her: "That'll be a tough act for you to follow, Miss Dietrich. Let's save that for the end. I think they'll wait!" That got the desired foot stomping and whistles. In a flash, Dietrich reappeared in her sequined sheath dress and wow! It really was Marlene, the screen goddess, who could be enjoying the luxuries of Hollywood but had come all the way to North Africa to entertain them, and the boys were on their feet cheering! She sang her famous songs. They loved her. She chose a boy from the audience to be the subject of Orson [Welles]'s mind-reading act. The boy stood there, gazing at her in the shimmering dress, she looked at him, then out at her audience: "When a GI looks at me, it's not hard to read his mind!" That was a sure laugh-getter. At the close of her act, she hiked up her dress, sat on a chair, put her musical saw between her legs, and played it! Pandemonium!5

Their shows followed this basic pattern wherever they performed. Dressed in a beautiful sequined dress, which had the advantage of not wrinkling in her small suitcase, Marlene dazzled the boys in olive green. While they were overawed that a beautiful, A-list Hollywood star would give up moviemaking to be with them, Marlene assured them that they were the best audience ever.

From Algiers, the troupe moved on to Italy, where they started performing shortly after Mussolini's overthrow. Conditions were primitive, with Marlene sometimes performing from the back of a truck. Without the benefit of stage lighting and backdrops it fell to the performers to carry the shows with just their hearts and voices. Marlene seemed very much alive in this environment. At some stops, up to 20,000 soldiers came to the shows, and while they loved all the performers, Marlene carried a special allure as she lulled them with her songs and cheered them with her jokes and good humor. On occasion, they decorated her field tent with local roses, trying to help her feel at ease. She made sure, on leaving, to take the roses with her so the men would know that she appreciated their gesture.[6]

In the course of many shows, Dietrich was on hand for some historical events. For example, she was the first entertainer to arrive in Anzio, Italy, after the Allied capture of Rome. And it was she who got to announce to the troops in Italy the momentous news that the Allies had landed at Normandy in northern France, signifying the long-awaited cross-channel invasion. This was on June 6, 1944, and it was not lost on Dietrich that the noose was starting to close on the Nazis.

Her first tour of duty a success, she returned to New York. In an interview with *Vogue* magazine reporter Leo Lerman, she described what it was like on the front lines, citing one of her many visits to a field Army hospital:

"'There are those rows of beds. In them, boys are sleeping or unconscious. Next to each bed stands a pole, and on that pole hangs a jar—a jar of blood. The only movement in that whole place is the bubbling blood, the only sound in that whole place is the bubbling blood, a little wisp of a sound . . . the only color in that place is the color of blood. You stand there with actual life running from bottles into the boys. You see it running into them. You hear it.'"[7]

Sometimes the American medical officers asked her to go talk with wounded German prisoners—a very poignant experience where this beautiful American movie star spoke to them in flawless German, offering words of comfort and support. Marlene Dietrich went to war with her eyes open—and provided comfort wherever the opportunity presented itself.

On her next USO tour she was with the troops as they advanced through France into Germany. It was heartrending on her return to Paris, a city she loved, to see how much the people had suffered. She performed shows to cheer up both civilian and military audiences. Then, she advanced with the troops on the front lines right into Germany. She was photographed at General Patton's side as he rallied his troops for the next round of assaults. At first, she was anxious as to how she would be received by the Germans, but the crowds were enthusiastic to have one of their own return home. She spoke to them in fluent German, and many asked her to speak well of them to their American conquerors.

Her efforts turned ominous when the German military surrounded Patton's Third Army Group at Bastogne in the Battle of the Bulge. Dietrich fully expected to be captured, and wondered what the Germans would do to her. Earlier, Patton had given her a handgun so she could protect herself, but the troops held out until the Germans retreated, and Dietrich was safe.

WORKING FOR THE OSS

In between her two USO tours, the OSS, precursor to the CIA, asked Dietrich to produce German-language propaganda radio broadcasts. In the Pacific Theater, a group of Japanese women played American songs that homesick GIs listened to on the radio. These women were collectively known as "Tokyo Rose," and they encouraged the American troops to surrender, given that the Japanese were triumphant everywhere.

In London, Marlene Dietrich played a similar role for the OSS by recording a number of German language radio programs that featured sentimental German songs intended to make the German military homesick and demoralized. The most popular was a German-language version of "Lili Marlene." So powerful was its effect that Joseph Goebbels, German Minister of Propaganda, banned listening to Dietrich's broadcasts because it undermined the defense of the homeland.

HONORED BY AMERICA

After the war ended, Marlene Dietrich went to Berlin to find her mother. She was overjoyed to find that Josefine had survived and the two had a tearful reunion. Her mother died a short time later, but at least they had found each other.

Returning to America, she made additional films, but by this point, she was a middle-aged female actress, which, at the time, was not a formula for success, and that was discouraging. She also found that while everyone admired the work she had done in the war, no one really wanted to talk about it. The country—and the world—was ready to move on, so this important chapter of her life became mostly a private memory. She did play an important role in the movie *Judgment at Nuremburg*, an indictment of Nazi war criminals. This was her final rebuke of the Nazis.

However, Marlene Dietrich was adaptable and resourceful. Once again she reinvented herself, creating a cabaret concert tour that took her around the country and to many other nations. In this way, she continued to earn the income needed to support Dietrich and her family.

Marlene Dietrich died on May 6, 1992, in her apartment in Paris. She was ninety years old, having lived a rich and sometimes scandalous life. But she was kind to the people she loved, worked hard for her fans, and placed her own life at risk for the cause of freedom.

In summing up her own life, she said that the most significant award of her life was receiving the Medal of Freedom in 1947 at the United States Military Academy at West Point.

Marlene Dietrich was hardly an invisible soldier—she lived most of her life in the spotlight, including her service in the USO during World War II. However, her individual acts of kindness to American GIs without the camera trained on her remained a private offering given from the heart. Sometimes GIs asked her to kiss the bandages on their wounded arms, which she did without hesitation. Her German-language propaganda broadcasts did not become known or appreciated until long after the war, even though they clearly had a negative impact on German morale.

So perhaps Marlene Dietrich is representative of the many talented Americans who supported the war in noncombat roles—raising money through the sale of war bonds, visiting soldiers in hospitals, and singing to the troops who were far away from home. While their acts do not find their way into the military history books, they still played a vital role in winning the war for freedom.

CHAPTER 4

JUAN PUJOL

THE ALLIES' MOST SUCCESSFUL DOUBLE AGENT

INTRODUCTION

To create a great novel, the author needs to create a compelling story that includes some very specific elements: A brave but quirky hero; an evil and dangerous villain; high stakes for the innocents who depend on the hero; high risk to the life and safety of the hero; and suspense—the outcome isn't known until late in the story, and at key points it will appear as if the hero has failed.

Who could guess that from 1941 to 1945 just such a story would be written, which was entirely fiction but which had the real-world consequence of deceiving Nazi Germany about the place and time of the D-Day landings at Normandy on June 6, 1944? A diminutive Spaniard is the hero of our story. He placed himself in great jeopardy as a double agent, deceiving the mighty

German Abwehr with a continuous feed of misinformation about the real facts of the invasion. Had his deception been discovered, the Germans could have moved three Panzer divisions and all available Luftwaffe aircraft to smash the invasion forces as they landed on the Normandy beaches.

But Juan Pujol was a clever man. He created some twenty-seven imaginary agents to give the appearance that he had an active spy network on task in sites across Great Britain. Along with other deception efforts, Pujol convinced the Germans that the D-Day landings were a diversion, not the real invasion. Because of his deception, Hitler withheld vital reinforcements until it was too late to turn the British and American forces back into the sea. So top-secret were Pujol's activities that his story remained classified for fifty years after the war ended. Though Juan Pujol was not the best-known fiction writer in history, it is very possible that his body of work saved more lives and had the greatest military impact in the real world of any work of fiction. He was a hero of World War II whose story is both intriguing and inspiring.

JUAN PUJOL (GARCIA)

"I had the idea that this man was a demon, a man who could completely destroy humanity. . . . I wanted to start a personal war with Hitler . . . and I wanted to fight with my imagination."—Juan Pujol[1]

Juan Pujol was born on February 28, 1912, in Barcelona, Spain. He occasionally included his mother's name, Garcia, to honor her. His father was the owner of a successful fabric dyeing company, which enabled Pujol to live a comfortable life prior to the Spanish Civil War that started in 1936. He adored his father and learned many important lessons from him about the value of individual liberty and respect for all people. "He taught me to respect the individuality of human beings, their sorrows and their sufferings. . . . He despised war and bloody revolutions, scorning the despot, the authoritarian."[2] Always high strung and imaginative, young Pujol put his restless energy to work learning five languages: Spanish, French, Catalan, Portuguese, and English. He had a vivid imagination and often envisioned himself as a Hollywood action hero. Growing up in Barcelona in the 1920s was risky, especially for the child of a factory owner. Labor discontent often led to strikes in which the lives of business owners were threatened. Political factions warred with each other, with frequent bloodshed, kidnapping, and murders. As a leading industrialist, Juan Pujol's father lived in daily fear for his life—so much so that he eventually moved his family out of the city to a safer suburb. Here the family felt more secure, although the future was still uncertain. As a teenager Pujol loved activity but became bored with his schoolwork. Eventually he dropped out and followed a course of self-study in the literary classics by reading the books in his father's extensive library. He described himself as undisciplined and a frequent source of concern and disappointment to his parents. This changed after a burst appendix nearly ended his life. Juan Pujol determined to settle down and pursue a vocation that would make his father proud of him. He was just finding success when a 1934 flu pandemic infected both he and his father. While Juan lay weakened by a fever, he heard screams from the room next door. His father's doctor had administered a dose of medicine that normally helped, but that killed his father the moment he emptied the syringe into his father's arm. Pujol was devastated: "The flight of his soul from the world left me oppressed and overwhelmed. I had lost the one I loved the most, for ever."[3]

After his father's death, Juan Pujol, now twenty-two, started a restless search for how best to occupy his life. He started several businesses, some with his older brother, but all failed. Eventually he became a salesman for a poultry farm and became engaged to marry. Then in 1936 the Spanish Civil War broke out and Pujol's life changed forever.

THE SPANISH CIVIL WAR

The Spanish Civil War is known to history as a particularly brutal coup by right-wing Nationalists under the leadership of General Francisco Franco who rose up to overthrow the Republican government that had been in power since 1931. How that intersects this story is that Juan Pujol determined that he would never kill another Spaniard. So rather than fight, he chose to go into hiding to avoid being conscripted by either the Republicans or the Nationalists. At first he hid in the home of his fiancée. But one day that refuge was raided by the police, who'd been tipped off that the family was hiding expensive jewelry and gold coins—which the police were there to confiscate. In their search they found Pujol and arrested him at gunpoint. He was put in jail with the very real threat of being executed as a deserter.

But after a week in jail, a secret Catholic group, the Socorro Blanco, alerted to his arrest by his longsuffering fiancée, arranged for his escape to a safe house. Then he shared a small apartment with the family of a taxi driver, having to live in secret so that neighbors would not betray him, although he was able to speak quietly with their nine-year-old son to help him with his math and other school assignments. After several close calls in which the police searched the apartment, the family decided to move out to the country, leaving Pujol alone in the apartment.

To avoid detection, he could not take the risk of starting a fire in the stove when it was cold or opening a window when it was hot. A young woman from the Socorro Blanco occasionally smuggled food into the apartment, but otherwise Pujol was on his own. After nearly a year in hiding, he was emaciated and haggard as well as demoralized by his solitary existence. Recognizing the depth of his depression, he realized he had to leave the apartment. The woman who had kept him alive managed to get hold of some forged identity papers so that he could reemerge into the world of the living.

He then had to find a way to exist in the world. He decided to escape to France or Portugal. Such a course was fraught with danger; first he had to join the Republican Army to find his way to the border. Then his plan was to slip through enemy lines and desert to the Nationalists, who were clearly winning the war at this point. If it sounds complicated, it was—because nearly everything that Juan Pujol did was complicated. It also set the stage for his later life as a double agent, pretending to be on one side while secretly supporting the other. When he finally made it to the front lines near the French border, the Republican troops he was serving with were close to starving, and the Nationalists just a few yards away taunted them, boasting about all the great food they had to eat. After learning the lay of the land, Pujol and two friends set a time to make their attempted escape. It was foolhardy in the extreme.

"Starving, disenchanted with life and longing for more congenial company, I decided to try to cross over to the 'enemy.' Looking back now I would never take such a hazardous risk again. To cross from Republican to Nationalist lines was the craziest thing I ever did in my long and adventurous existence. About seven o'clock on a clear, moonlit evening, three of us prepared to desert. I took two hand grenades for reassurance, although I had no intention of using them, but before I could slip out of my trench, my two companions jumped clumsily out of theirs and started a landslide of small pebbles that clattered as they rolled down the rocky hillside. A sentry heard the noise and raised the alarm. I hesitated for a moment and then started off, hotly pursued by a patrol. Confused, I made for a patch of pine trees, where I tried to hide. In no time I had completely lost my sense of direction, but I carried on and began to climb up the hill. Unfortunately, I was climbing up the very hill I had just come down, straight back into my own lines. When I realized my error, I turned and raced back down the hill again, dodging the bursts of gunfire; taking huge strides, half sliding, half leaping, I soon reached the bottom, where I went to ground in a reed bed. I could hear the voices of the patrol hunting for me, thrusting the butts of their rifles into the reeds, rightly guessing me to be close by. After about fifteen minutes I heard them change direction, so I crept out of the reeds as quietly as I could and dashed up the hill—the right one this time—into a belt of pines. I found a shallow ditch about the width of my body and slid in, covering myself over with leaves and twigs. I could have thrown my two hand grenades at the Republican patrol who were only a few feet below me, but my conscience held me back: although I was desperate, I recoiled at the carnage.

"The patrol stopped for a smoke and, just before some rain clouds obscured the moon, I caught a glimpse of their silhouettes, they were so close. There were six of them. I lay there shaking with fear and covered in sweat, waiting for them to return to their lines. As soon as I heard the Nationalists start their customary evening banter, 'Hey, Reds, what've they given you to eat today?' I decided to move, using their voices as a guide. I took off my boots, so as to get a better grip on the slippery gravel slope and left them and my hand grenades in the ditch. Slowly, taking great care, I began to clamber up the hill, across some terraced fields and over a couple of walls. Suddenly, I heard voices very close. I got such a fright, I must have passed out, for phrases seemed to echo through my head as if in a nightmare: 'Don't worry now, lad' and 'We're coming to you.' Recovering, I raced to the top where I found my two companion escapers. They'd made it across in a matter of minutes, while I was exhausted, hungry and bleeding. They told me that when the Republicans started firing, the rebels had asked them what was going on and they had said that there was a third person out there trying to escape. Whereupon the rebels had begun their nightly exchange of views while they sent out a patrol to search for me, presuming I had got lost.

"For two days we slept in our new trenches and ate and ate. When another escapee joined us, he told us that the Republican patrol had eventually found the ditch where I'd been hiding and had discovered my boots and hand grenades. It had been a wild and suicidal idea to escape and I swore never to embark on anything so dangerous again '. . . world without end. Amen.'"[4]

Pujol and his friends were arrested by the Nationalists and sent to prison to make sure they were not simply pretending to be deserters to act as double agents. It was here that Pujol put his writing skills to work for the first time, selling an expensive pen his father had given him so he could buy a less expensive pen as well as paper, ink, and postage. He started writing letters to everyone he knew, asking for them to intervene in his behalf. Eventually a Catholic priest, an old friend of his father's, showed up at the camp and vouched for Pujol. He was granted leave to join up with a regular Nationalist unit.

By now the Nationalists were winning the war and slowly closing in on Madrid. Although Pujol was sent to the front on one occasion, he managed to keep his commitment to himself to never kill another Spaniard. He later wrote, "I had managed not to fire a single bullet by the time Madrid fell a few months later, bringing the war to an end."[5] More than one million Spaniards were killed in the war and the country was to spend the next thirty-six years under the iron rule of the leader of the Nationalists, General Franco.

AN AGENT FOR GERMANY—AN AGENT FOR BRITAIN

By 1941 Juan Pujol had fallen in love and married a nurse who had cared for him after an injury in the army. She had a feisty temperament and loved to socialize. Pujol struggled to earn enough money to support their desired lifestyle. He also wrestled with his conscience regarding Nazi Germany. While Spain and Portugal were both neutral in the war between the Axis and Allied powers, General Franco allowed the Nazis relatively unfettered travel within Spanish territory. The Nazis used this advantage to set up an extensive spy network.

"The German embassy in Madrid was a hive of Nazi intelligence; it employed 391 people, 220 of whom were full-time Abwehr officers, split into sections for espionage, counterespionage and sabotage. These officers directed 1,500 agents spread all over Spain, who in turn had their own informers and subagents. The communications of this gargantuan network kept a staff of 34 radio operators busy around the clock sending coded messages to Abwehr headquarters in Berlin, by way of Paris. The Abwehr apparatus in Spain was directed with the knowledge and approval of Franco, who was well aware that Spain was honeycombed with Nazi spies."[6]

Pujol hated the Nazis. As early as 1934 he had heard rumors about the arrest and detention of Jews, and even darker rumors that they were being executed on a mass scale. This troubled him so deeply that he eventually decided to approach the British embassy to offer himself as a spy for the Allies. Unfortunately, when he showed up with no experience in espionage, no connections to the Germans living in Spain, and no one to recommend him, his offer was refused. Despondent, he confided his failure to his wife, Araceli. She offered to approach the British with a similar offer, but she too was turned down. The British were reluctant to do anything to provoke Spain into joining the war on the side of Germany, so they were not willing to take a risk on this young and inexperienced couple, no matter how eager they were to serve.

Regrouping, Juan and Araceli decided that they had to find something of value to offer the British—real information that could be used against the Germans. To do so, they would have to cultivate contacts with local Germans. And what better way to do that than to offer to become German spies working for the Abwehr against Britain! If they could infiltrate the German spy network, they would gain insider knowledge that might prove useful to the Allies. Of course, the role of double agent is far more hazardous than that of even a spy since there are so many stories to keep straight, and so many chances for betrayal. But to truly help defeat Germany without taking up arms, this seemed the only path available.

The first step in this audacious plan was to stop thinking like a Spaniard who hated the Nazis and start thinking like a Spaniard who was enamored of the Nazis. That was the only way Pujol could convince the Abwehr to sign him up. He and Araceli started reading everything they could about Nazi ideology and prominent Nazi leaders. Once he felt he knew enough to pull off the deception, Pujol requested a meeting with the German embassy. He was assigned to a man with whom he would become close for the next four years, the Spanish-born son of a German businessman.

His handler's code name was Federico, and his job was to recruit and train spies. Federico also thought of himself as a skilled interrogator who could sniff out a potential double agent. At their first meeting he asked Pujol exactly what he wanted to do for the Abwehr and why he thought he was qualified to do so. A little nervous, Pujol excitedly told Federico how much he hated the Allies and how much he admired the Nazis; he wanted to be on the winning side of the war by helping in the clandestine activities that were part of every war. Pujol made up the names of prominent British politicians and embassy personnel that he supposedly knew on both a professional and personal basis.

He was an enthusiastic salesman, but could tell from Federico's flat response that he was not doing well, so he turned the volume up even higher. When Federico brought the interview to an end, Pujol thought that he had failed. But he was surprised when the Abwehr agent requested a follow-up meeting. What he had not counted on was that many Germans, and Federico in particular, had a hackneyed view of Spaniards as emotional, excitable, and expressive, exactly what Pujol had displayed. Federico had overlooked Pujol's hyperbole and wanted to learn more.

After several more meetings in which Pujol promised far more than he could legitimately deliver, the Germans offered him a job. He was to be trained as an Abwehr agent, fully skilled at using invisible ink to convey his messages to the Abwehr in Madrid. He was given the code name Alaric, and his fictional network of spies was named *Arabel*, which translates to "answered prayer."

At this point, Pujol was in a predicament. He had promised the Germans that he could provide them meaningful intelligence gleaned from conversations with high ranking British embassy personnel as well as lower-level contacts. But how to do that when he did not know any British living in Spain? The answer took three forms.

First, he decided to go to Lisbon, Portugal, where British commercial flights and oceangoing vessels could still arrive and depart. He had forged a Spanish diplomatic passport earlier, which allowed him relatively unfettered travel anywhere in the world that was not directly involved in the war, so passage into Portugal was now open to him. He figured that it would be easier for him to gather information there that he could use to spice up his false reports with valid information. And it would put him beyond the direct supervision of the Abwehr in Madrid.

Second, once he was in Portugal, he pretended to move to England. This was a big stretch, since he had never been to England. He bought a travel book and railway timetable that gave him maps and names of public buildings, restaurants, clubs, and pubs in London. From this, he pretended to set up residence in England's capital city and to develop a network of spies in London and in other cities in the United Kingdom. This was his most audacious move by far, since it is difficult to speak authentically about a place you have never seen, let alone purport to be living in at the time.

Third, Pujol simply made things up. He used his rich imagination to start building a fictional network of contacts in both England and Portugal that he could cite in his reports to the Abwehr. His goal was to divert their attention away from legitimate British activities and to thus aid the British war effort. Remarkably, even though he had *no* contacts, he started filing reports that were accepted and believed by the Abwehr. Many were of little consequence—he might report on seeing a particular British ship in port, or about imaginary troop movements into or out of the city. He sometimes discussed a supposedly overheard conversation in a portside tavern.

One of the early problems Pujol had to overcome was explaining why his reports to Abwehr Madrid were postmarked from Lisbon—after all, he was supposed to be living in England. With his usual creativity he overcame this problem by reporting that he had made friends with a Royal Dutch KLM Airlines attendant who flew the London-to-Lisbon route. Pujol said that he had persuaded this fictional friend to post letters for him from Lisbon since that would raise far less suspicion than letters mailed from London. To his great relief Federico accepted this explanation.

In the beginning, none of his reports were actionable, something that the Germans could confirm and use in combat against the British. But all that took a dramatic turn when he invented a troop convoy that was to sail from Liverpool, England, to the island of Malta in the Mediterranean. What Pujol did not learn until later is that a real British convoy sailed on a similar date and route as his fictional convoy. Even more important from a British point of view was that the Germans acted on the Arabel network's report by diverting U-boats from their regular patrols to intercept Pujol's phony convoy. Only luck kept them from striking the real convoy.

Pujol was a success—the diversion saved British lives because of changed German plans. And the passage of a real convoy convinced the Germans that Alaric (Pujol) was legitimate. But that is not the most intriguing part of the story—it was this incident that led to the most important development in Pujol's private war against Adolf Hitler.

DRIVING THE BRITISH CRAZY

The British government was far better prepared than the Germans with respect to double agents operating inside England. In fact, by 1941 the British had searched out and discovered every single German agent operating inside the United Kingdom. Some had been killed while being arrested. Most had been turned by the British into double agents who continued to collect a paycheck from the Abwehr while actually working under the strict supervision of the British intelligence services. For the double agent it was a better choice than execution.

But then in late 1941 and early 1942 Juan Pujol's Arabel spy network appeared on radio intercepts between the Abwehr in Madrid and their headquarters in Berlin. From the nature of the reports it appeared that the leader, Alaric, was living somewhere in England, although there were some nonsensical elements to his transmissions that made it hard to believe he was really in the country. If there was a German agent, he had to be found and either turned or arrested. Of course, it was impossible to find Alaric in England since Pujol was living in secrecy in Lisbon. A convoluted situation, to be sure.

For his part, Juan Pujol was getting discouraged. While in Portugal he'd lived apart from Araceli and he missed her. And after the convoy incident, the Abwehr started making fewer requests of him, which suggested that his invented reports were not as valuable as the Germans had hoped it would be. Pujol later wrote that he felt the time was fast approaching when he should give up the game and move somewhere else—perhaps to South America—to avoid recriminations by the Abwehr. But before taking that last step Pujol decided that he'd make one last attempt to work for the Allies. He went to the American embassy in Lisbon in early February 1942 and asked to speak to either the military or naval attaché.

"I began to unburden myself by telling him about my attempt to contact the British in Madrid, my rejection and then my resolution, fired by *amour-propre* [self-respect], to obtain some practical and useful information that would capture their imagination, vindicate my humiliation and enhance myself in their estimation so that they would believe that I was motivated by a desire to defend democracy. I briefly outlined my contacts with the Germans and mentioned that they had given me invisible ink, a code book and money; I told him about my trip to Portugal, my second attempt to contact the British through their Lisbon embassy, my second rebuff, my resolution to press on with work begun and, finally, my last desperate move of coming to see him; I said that if that too failed, then all the work I had done so far would come to naught.

"Demorest [the attaché] showed keen interest right from the very beginning and seemed amazed by my story. He asked me for proof, which I proceeded to give him. For the first time there seemed to be a distinct possibility that I had found the right person; at last, someone was going to help me to complete the mission I had set myself.

"It was precisely while I was telling him my story that its full implication struck me: I started to realize the potential value of the trick I had begun to play on the Third Reich.

"Demorest asked for two days in which to follow up my story, confer with his British colleagues and convince them that they must get in touch with me. He gave me his phone number and urged me to be very careful and to avoid going out unless I had to. Then Demorest evidently tried to make his British counterpart, Captain

Benson, see that he had nothing to lose by telling his superiors that this alleged agent wanted to hand over some invisible ink and a code book, and he advised Benson that he must act swiftly as I had either to continue with the game or stop altogether. Someone in England had already had the perception to suspect that the spy they were hunting for was probably the same person as the freelance agent at large in Portugal, so some days later Captain Benson asked Demorest to give me his phone number.

"I then telephoned Benson, who arranged for me to meet . . . an MI6 officer in Lisbon. . . . Three days later [he] telephoned me to say that he had received instructions that I should be taken to London."[7]

After all his failed attempts to connect with the British, he was finally on his way to England. It is unclear if the primary motive of the British was simply to take a German agent out of action or to accept Pujol's offer of service. They had to be careful that they were not taking in a German double agent—one who would betray them at a crucial moment. Once in England, the task of deciding whether to accept Pujol fell primarily to Tomas ("Tommy") Harris of MI5.

Harris was an accomplished artist whose mother was Spanish and whose father was English and Jewish. His father owned and operated a successful Spanish art gallery in London, which gave him connections to his father's influential patrons. Tomas had been educated in Spain and spoke flawless Spanish. His biggest obstacle in accepting Pujol into MI5's mission was his astonishment at the sheer audacity of what Pujol had tried to pull off on the Germans. After determining that Pujol was sincere, Harris and other leaders in MI5 had to decide if they could successfully manage the incredible imagination of this young Spaniard who had taken it onto himself to deceive the Nazis with nothing more than a British travel guide and a railway schedule. Would he be able to maintain the deception over time?

Ultimately, after numerous interviews, Pujol was accepted, and Tommy Harris became his daily handler for the remainder of the war. Together they created a portfolio of fictional agents operating in towns as far north as Scotland and in all the major industrial ports and cities of England. It was a highly productive collaboration. When it was time to find a code name for Pujol, the British chose "Garbo," a reference to Greta Garbo, the most famous actress in the world at the time. Naming their agent after Garbo paid homage to Pujol's superb acting skills as well as creating confusion as to whether this agent was a male or female. From that point forward Pujol's English network was identified as Operation Garbo. Thus he was Alaric and Arabel for the Abwehr, and Garbo for MI5.

In May 1943, the British arranged for Juan Pujol's wife and young son to travel from Madrid to England to join him. Pujol was now out of harm's way in Portugal, but his life was still in danger if the Germans ever discovered that he was working for the British; it is almost certain they would have sent an assassin to kidnap and kill him. He was playing a high stakes game that could substantially impact the unfolding of the war in Europe.

GARBO AND HARRIS CREATE A SPY NETWORK

The first task for Tommy Harris was to sort out the many fictional characters that Pujol had created while in Portugal, including their nonexistent addresses in various parts of the United Kingdom. When writing fiction, it is not enough to simply create a character—the author must create a constellation of people that interact with each of the major characters. Remarkably, Pujol had done this for many of his invented agents but had kept their intersecting stories in his head. Relying on memory alone increased the chance of making a "reference mistake," with each added character and each fictional mission completed adding to the risk.

Harris went to work creating a folder for each of Pujol's main characters and creating an organizational chart to show the relationships between Pujol and each of his characters. Into these folders went reports previously sent to the Abwehr about the fictional agent, including references to the people in their lives who could influence their success a field operative. Some were married, others were bachelors or single women. All had jobs to give them cover while spying for Germany in England. Each had to have a reason to turn against England and support the Nazis—for some it was ideology, for others an insult or sleight at work. A fair number of his characters were unknowingly being used by Pujol's network; they were loyal to England, but talked too freely after a few too many drinks at the pub. A few were even made to be a bit unreliable, the intelligence they provided Pujol transmitted with a note of skepticism. All of this was to make it seem as if Pujol were working with real people, including all the complications that go with everyday life. In every case the character had to be believable so that the Germans would treat their information as worthy of consideration.

Eventually, Pujol and Harris created a total of seven primary agents and twenty other minor informants whom the Germans believed reported to "Alaric" as head of the Arabel network. To provide authenticity to the reports these agents filed, MI5 hired a location scout to travel through England and fill in details about the various locations where the agents were supposedly living, including such small details as ice cream shops where they could get a treat, or hotels near military bases where an agent would meet informants.

After identifying the characters, Harris and his team then went through the thirty-eight messages Pujol had previously sent to Federico to sort them out and, in essence, create a "character bible" that included the physical characteristics of the agents, their locations, their areas of expertise, and the reports they had previously filed.

With this framework in place, MI5 began the task of using Garbo's network to deceive the Germans. The first step, ironically, was to send them accurate but unimportant military information. By moving to England and teaming up with MI5, Pujol now had access to accurate information that would confirm his authenticity. Each week the XX Committee—the high-level group responsible for all British counterintelligence operations—would send Harris new authentic information that Pujol and Harris could work into the letters they posted to Federico in Madrid.

While living in Portugal, Pujol had posted his reports to Madrid himself. But he had made the Abwehr believe that they were being posted by either a fictional KLM pilot (who posted them for free as a favor to his drinking buddy Pujol) or by his second air courier, the KLM steward, whom Pujol paid to post the letters. After moving to Britain, MI5 continued the deception by engaging one of their Lisbon-based agents to post the letters. To the Abwehr nothing had changed—the letters from England were posted in Lisbon to Madrid by the KLM pilot or steward, just as it had always been. The truth was that an active MI5 agent had replaced Pujol.

But it was not as easy it sounds; the posting of the letters had to be done on a strictly monitored schedule. Since the days and times of the flights between London and Lisbon were known to the Germans, Pujol and Harris had to be very careful that a letter wasn't posted while the fictional KLM pilot or the steward was supposed to be in England on a turnaround. This was complicated by the fact that the pilot and steward often flew on different days! To add even greater authenticity, some letters were sent directly to Madrid with a London postmark (since Spain was still neutral) to prove that Pujol was living in England as he said. Hardest of all is that the intelligence in these letters was painstakingly written in invisible ink between lines of regular ink to deceive the British censors in Lisbon and Madrid.

Once assisted by MI5, Pujol's reports increased in frequency and accuracy. The goal was to convince the Germans that Pujol was in charge of their most reliable network in England. As his Garbo network grew, the reports grew longer and more detailed. During the war Pujol and Harris sent more than 350 letters to Madrid, many more than 2,000 words in length, and all written painstakingly in invisible ink so they could get past the censors.

"Garbo's 'agents' were now roaming all over the country, and their reports read like a spy's Baedeker [travel guide] of small towns and harbors: 'The beach here is mined. There is a very large gun in Singleton Park, but I could not find out if it is for A.A. [antiaircraft] or coastal defenses. . . . Several large aircraft hangars. 15 barrage balloons—A.A. placed to the north and west of the aerodrome. Many sentries. . . . The small port of Irvine is now being used for assault barges. I saw ten anchored.'"[8]

In this reporting, Pujol also included personal details about the agents who supposedly filed the report. In one case, an agent's sister became suspicious of his time away from home. Another's wife was jealous of his socializing. Spouses would often complain about not having enough money, so Pujol would request an even larger draw from the Abwehr for that agent, and so on.

While much of the task of creating reports now fell to professional writers at MI5, Juan Pujol continued playing an active role to make sure the reports were consistently in his style and that the fictional agents were the type that the Germans would expect him to recruit. One of his greatest fictional coups involved Pujol befriending a senior official at the Ministry of Information in London. The cover story went that Pujol had done translation work for this official who asked him to have a drink together. They bonded over Pujol's memories of the Spanish Civil War, which had been observed by the official. To the Germans, the ministry official remained a loyal subject of king and country, and therefore an unconscious collaborator (the very highest value since his information would not be manipulated). Because it was plausible, the Germans accepted that this official existed and had really befriended Pujol.

Perhaps the easiest way to explain Pujol's fictional network is to briefly look at each of his seven agents and twenty contacts. Agent 1 was the KLM steward, "Smith," who died in 1943. He carried correspondence for Pujol to Lisbon, bypassing the British censors. His motive was the payments he received for doing so, justifying his conscience with the thought that Pujol was a political refugee, so forwarding his correspondence was not harmful to England. Later, he became a more sinister player, facilitating money laundering between Portugal and England. On the positive side, Smith helped Pujol recruit four other important contacts: (1) a KLM pilot and courier who helped Pujol report his first intelligence from Britain, antiaircraft batteries deployed in Hyde Park; (2) the head of the Catalan section of the British Ministry of Information; (3) a censor in the Ministry of Information; and (4) a female secretary working for the British Cabinet who became infatuated with Pujol, even though he remained faithful to his wife. She was a flirtatious character who became indiscreet when she and Pujol went out for drinks. In this way she unwittingly passed important information to Pujol, including information about the 1943 Moscow conference. Since the Germans had other knowledge of this conference, this helped secure their confidence in Pujol's network.

Smith and the four contacts he brought to the Arabel network provided Pujol with a means of communication with the Abwehr and anecdotal access to the highest levels of British government. All added a great deal of credibility to Pujol's reports.

The story took an interesting twist when Smith supposedly discovered that Pujol was really a German agent and blackmailed him for £2,200 to prevent him from exposing Pujol to the British. The Germans were happy to pay since it made Pujol more dependent on them. In this way MI5 extracted an additional £2,200 payment from the Germans to help fund the cost of the Operation Garbo network. Because Agent 1's story was difficult maintain, he was reported to have died in 1943.

Agent 2 was William Gerbers, a Swiss-German businessman who died in 1942. After his death Pujol persuaded the Germans to provide his widow a lifetime pension in exchange for relatively low-level information that she could provide—even more money from Berlin to pay for London to spy on them.

Agent 3, "Carlos" (given the German code name Benedict), was a Venezuelan student living in Glasgow. His story was that he hated the British for disrupting Spanish culture in South America. He played a central role in feeding Adolf Hitler's paranoia that the British intended to invade Norway from Scotland. Carlos added three others to his network (none of whom knew they were helping the Germans), including a pilot officer, an officer in the British 49th Infantry, and a Greek seaman who had deserted.

Agent 4 was Chamillus—a Gibraltarian who worked at the Navy, Army, Air Force Institutes (NAAFI), a service organization that provided recreational activities and sundries to members of the British military awaiting deployment. In this role Chamillus was in an ideal position to overhear lots of loose talk from servicemen relative to their location, troop strength, areas of specialty, and so forth. He enlisted the aid of three others, including "Almura," a radio operator who freed Pujol from sending written reports by post, a guard based in Chislehurst (a London suburb), and a US NCO based in London. Chamillus was one of Pujol's most influential fictional creations.

Agent 5 was "Moonbeam"—Carlos's Venezuelan brother who lived in Ottawa, Canada. Moonbeam also had help from a cousin who lived in Buffalo, New York. This gave Arabel an international reach that further delighted the Abwehr.

Agent 6 was a British field security NCO who died in 1943.

Agent 7 was "Dagobert," an ex-seaman living in Swansea, Wales. Dagobert created the most extensive subnetwork for Pujol, enlisting the help of seven others including: Donny (leader of the World Aryan Order); Wren, who lived on the island of Ceylon; Dick, an Indian fanatic who hated the British for occupying his country; Drake, who lived in Exeter; a Welsh fascist who lived in South Wales; and Dorick, who lived in Harwich by the North Sea.

Whew! The Arabel network was complicated, with intricate storylines. It is hard to write about these people without subconsciously thinking they must have been real. But they were not—all were Juan Pujol's inventions fleshed out by Tommy Harris and his team to serve two primary purposes:

First, to feed the Germans important misinformation at key points in the war, most notably in the buildup to the D-Day invasion of Europe at Normandy. It was vital that the Germans believed that they had credible sources within England that could verify that the actual invasion was to take place near Pas-de-Calais rather than at Normandy. This was Operation Garbo's primary objective and reason for being.

Second, to create a "reverse telescope" to discern what the Germans were thinking and what they worried about. In other words, Operation Garbo was not just a one-way street with Pujol passively sending on information. The Abwehr gave the Arabel network specific assignments to seek out information that was important to them. By analyzing these requests, the British could discern patterns that told them what Germany was thinking.

For example, in the early days of the war, when the Abwehr requested details about grocery stores and food supply depots near Devon, it indicated they wanted to know how to secure food for their troops after the invasion Hitler was planning with Operation Sealion. About a year later, these requests faded, indicating that the invasion was off as Hitler shifted his focus to invading Russia. The reverse telescope is also how Britain learned that Adolf Hitler was concerned about an Allied invasion of Norway, which prompted the British to disseminate misinformation suggesting that such an invasion was imminent. The Germans were forced to keep troops and equipment in Norway rather than redeploying them to the Russian front or to the French coastline. The telescope also confirmed that the German high command believed that the Allied invasion was to take place at Calais, making it easier to feed this false belief with reports from Garbo and other double agents.

In both these objectives Operation Garbo was successful. But it is surprising how it had to play out. For example, the British would often feed legitimate and potentially damaging information to the Germans to reinforce their trust in Pujol's reports. Whenever possible, however, the British would time those reports so that the Germans wouldn't have time to act on the intelligence in a meaningful way. They had to play all this close to the edge—potentially putting Allied lives at risk—in order to maintain credibility for the largest deception of all, the eventual invasion of mainland Europe.

One of the first incidents in which Pujol succeeded in altering future German policy came about after a German fighter aircraft shot down KLM Flight 777 while en route to Lisbon from London. The world-famous actor Leslie Howard of *Gone with the Wind* fame was on board the flight and was killed with everyone else aboard. When the German fighter crew later boasted publicly that they had shot down the unarmed passenger airliner for nothing more than "target practice," Pujol wrote a scathing letter to Federico saying that this foolish and provocative act had endangered his most reliable means of transmitting letters, and had turned up the heat on all foreigners living in England. He strongly advised that this never happen again. The Germans did investigate and, while they did not discipline the pilot who shot down the airliner, there was never again an attack on KLM flights.

This was a crucial success to the British intelligence service who needed to maintain this quick and direct contact with a neutral country. Pujol's pushback against the Germans in this incident was also a good example of how he sometimes cajoled the Germans and other times bullied them. He always kept up the persona of a highly emotional agent constantly afraid for both his own safety and his wife and son's—as well as the agents who reported to him. He made it seem to the Abwehr that he was often on the brink of quitting, which kept the Germans off-balance in their relationship. In this light, his outburst about Flight 777 was consistent, believable, and likely led to a change in Luftwaffe policy.

GARBO REPORTS ON OPERATION TORCH

With more than 350 written reports and hundreds more coded radio transmissions later in the war, Operation Garbo involved thousands of intelligence transmissions to the Germans—so many that it is impossible to sum them up neatly. Rather, here is one example of one of his earliest and most consequential deception campaigns that demonstrates how the program worked to both inform and deceive the Germans.

Operation Torch was planned in late 1942 as the Allies' first major attempt to bring America into the war in a way that would take pressure off the Russian front. Because Churchill was adamant that they were not yet ready for an invasion of mainland Europe, it was decided that a US Army group under the command of General George S. Patton would attack the Germans in North Africa near Casablanca. It was to be a massive undertaking, with more than 107,000 American and British troops landing on beaches more than 2,000 miles from England or America. It was really a make-or-break proposition. Here's how Garbo helped:

Playing to Adolf Hitler's fears of an invasion of Norway, the Garbo network first played up the idea that large numbers of troops were training in western Scotland for seaborne landings. The Germans would infer based on their worries that this training was meant for a move against Norway. To add authenticity, the British carried out actual bombing raids against German facilities in Norway across the North Sea as the day of the real invasion in Africa approached.

As the Africa date drew near, Garbo's network began to report that there were troops collecting farther south, including Liverpool, who were dressed for Mediterranean operations. Providing this authentic detail was essential to maintaining Garbo's credibility. But the intelligence that Garbo passed along suggested that the operation in Africa was most likely planned for Dakar in West Africa, nearly 1,000 miles from the actual landing zones. Thus, the Germans had to prepare for two possible invasions—one which was *not* to come in Norway and one which *would* come, but far from where the Germans were prepared to fight.

In executing his deception campaign for Operation Torch, Garbo had a problem with Agent 2, the Swiss-German businessman William Gerber, who had been credited with reporting the convoy to Malta that had brought Pujol into the British system. It would be impossible for Gerber to not notice all the troops assembling in Liverpool earlier than Garbo planned to report about them. Gerber's failure to report this buildup was likely to discredit Pujol in the Abwehr's eyes.

Early in the planning Pujol had to take Gerber out of action. First, he reported to Federico that Gerber had taken ill—so ill that Pujol had made an urgent trip to Liverpool to see him. He reported that Gerber's wife was frantic when he got there, so Pujol had arranged for his immediate transfer to a hospital to treat a mysterious undiagnosed illness. Tommy Harris consulted with medical doctors to come up with a list of symptoms that were real enough to deceive. Not long later, Pujol reported that to his great sorrow William Gerber had died. At the same time, he reported that he had recruited three new agents, but that none of them were in Liverpool. Thus, his network was blind, for the moment, with respect to that key military port.

The deception was remarkable in its complexity:

"On October 11, 1942, Garbo informed Madrid that 'No. 6 tells me that rumors are circulating among journalists that the objective will be Dakar.' . . . Garbo immediately qualified the news by telling Madrid that the war correspondents were in the pocket of the War Ministry, and thus Dakar was probably a false target. He was creating a smokescreen composed of many gray shades.

"As the invasion approached, the XX Committee pushed Garbo up to a new level of prominence. They had to sprinkle enough trust in his messages to keep the Germans from suspecting him of disloyalty. One of his agents was allowed to 'see' one of the actual convoys leaving the river Clyde for French North Africa on October 27. Garbo quickly flashed the sighting to Madrid. Four days later, he sent another bulletin; more troops were being loaded onto battleships, and the camouflage was in Mediterranean colors: 'None of the troops with Arctic uniforms and equipment embarked as they are still here.' Garbo was beginning to suggest that Norway was a feint. The invasion was heading toward Africa. Finally, the pièce de résistance: while visiting with his Ministry of Information source, Garbo claimed he sneaked into the unsuspecting man's office and stole a look at a 'Most Secret' file titled 'Policy—French North Africa.' 'It was impossible for me, in the few moments available, to get more details. Nevertheless, I am convinced . . . that they are preparing propaganda which would come into force at the moment of an attack against these places.'

"Garbo had 'found' the target. On November 1, 1942, he banged out a letter warning the Germans that the Allies would hit North Africa. It was precisely the intelligence the Germans wanted from their top spy. That message would give them the upper hand at Casablanca and Algiers—the landing areas for the invasion—and hundreds if not thousands of Allied lives would be lost. *But MI5 ensured that Garbo's letter took days to pass through the British censors, so it arrived in Lisbon on November 9, one day too late.* It proved Garbo's worth without costing any lives.

"On [November 8th], American forces had stormed ashore at Casablanca after pounding the French Vichy batteries with their naval guns. . . . Within seventy-two hours, Casablanca was in Patton's hands. . . .

"When Federico finally opened Garbo's letter of November 1, here in his hands were all the details of a major Allied invasion, written *a week* before it happened. The Germans were crestfallen, but hugely impressed: 'Your last reports are all magnificent,' Federico wrote."[9]

The Germans had been misdirected, and yet Pujol's final report made it appear that his network had figured out and urgently reported on the truth. His stock was never higher with the Nazis—and it was because of operations like this that he would be taken seriously a year and a half later when the invasion of Europe occurred.

OPERATION FORTITUDE: DECEPTION PRIOR TO D-DAY

Operation Garbo was just one of many players in the massive deception effort codenamed "Operation Fortitude" that the Allies employed to confuse the Germans about where and when the invasion of Europe was to take place. The primary objective was to keep the German Panzer tank divisions away from the Normandy beaches for as long as possible so that enough Allied troops could establish a beachhead. One senior military planner asked for at least three days, believing that after that they could never be dislodged.

But while Operation Garbo was just one player in the disinformation campaign, reports after the war suggest that Pujol's deception was decisive in causing Hitler to order tanks that had been dispatched toward Normandy to turn around and go back to Pas-de-Calais for more than a week. Countless Allied lives were saved by this, and the credit goes to the idealist from Madrid and the team that was built up to support him. One field commander suggested that Garbo's assistance was worth more than a full division of 25,000 troops—high praise for one double agent.

Here is how the planners of Operation Fortitude proceeded to achieve their primary objectives of keeping the Germans tied down in Norway and at Pas-de-Calais.

First they created confusion by inventing Fortitude North and Fortitude South. Fortitude North was another ruse to convince Germany that Norway was to be the first stepping-stone into Europe. Fortitude South was planned to suggest that two invasions would take place in France: the first a small diversionary strike against the Normandy beaches that would precede the second main attack across the English Channel at Pas-de-Calais, the shortest route available to the Allies and therefore most desirable from a military point of view. Including Normandy was essential since it would be impossible to hide all the troops and ships massed for the real invasion. With three potential targets, the Germans had to prepare to defend thousands of miles of coast not knowing where the real blow would fall, and in the process stretch their supply lines and troop concentrations.

Supporting this primary objective was a massive effort to create false images of large numbers of troops and equipment being assembled across the English Channel from Calais using decoys and dummies, phony radio traffic, and "firsthand reports" from Pujol's imaginary agents. These deceptions had to portray that these troop concentrations were greater than the actual troops massing in the ports of Portland, Portsmouth, and Southampton in advance of the Normandy landings.

In practice, these fictional reports were almost always a mix of authentic and false information. They never did declare definitively where the main attack would be. Rather, the reports would provide a shifting array of suggestions such as, "The invasion looks like it will be in the north from Scotland," then, a week or so later, "It appears that Pas-de-Calais is the most likely," and finally, as the day approached, "It might be Normandy—but maybe not—it still looks like the main force is assembled for Calais." In other words, the Allies never declared that Pas-de-Calais *was* the intended target. Instead, they kept things up in the air so that the Germans had to keep guessing. Operation Garbo along with two other networks sent a flood of information to the Germans to overwhelm their military analysts. Just as real spies working in the shadows would struggle to form a true and complete picture, the information from the double agents was piecemeal and confusing. In the case of the Garbo group, all of it was orchestrated by Tommy Harris and Juan Pujol.

Since it is already established that Garbo was successful, let's cut to a few of the most decisive moments in his role in the D-Day invasion.

On May 29, 1944, exactly eight days prior to D-Day, Garbo's agent Donny (the leader of the fictional World Aryan Order) transmitted firsthand accounts of aircraft massing in the areas of Kent and Sussex in southeast England. This was followed by a massive attack against German bases in the Pas-de-Calais area by the Royal Air Force. Since the Germans knew full well they were being attacked, that was not the deception. But reporting accurately on numerous aircraft assembling in eastern England supported the story that Donny was on-site and that this bombing was a prequel to the main assault being directed against Calais. The reality was that after the softening-up attacks at Calais, these aircraft were held at these airfields until the last possible moment before being redeployed to support the Normandy landings a week later. By this point in the war the German Luftwaffe was fully engaged at the Russian front, so Donny's report posed little threat to these airfields, but Operation

Garbo gained credibility by appearing to be on the scene, yet with no risk to the lives of the aviators.

Several weeks earlier Harris and Pujol had gone all the way up the line of command to General Eisenhower to secure permission to broadcast that Allied ships were departing for Normandy three hours before the actual landings, on whatever day that turned out to be. They viewed this is an important way for Pujol to establish credibility so that they could be on record warning the Germans. It shows how much confidence the Allied command had in the operation that permission was granted. Much to their frustration, when their radio operator tried to connect with Madrid at 0300 hours on June 6, 1944, no one was there to receive them. It wasn't until 0800 that Madrid finally connected, and by then they were aware of the landings in France. This frustrated Pujol. So he came up with a clever plan. He immediately sent a message indicating that after the Normandy landings things seemed very quiet everywhere else in the country. He congratulated his agent Chamillus for providing advanced warning of the invasion at 0300 so that the German high command was notified what was coming. In other words, he pretended that he did not yet know that Madrid had not answered until 0800. Shortly after that, he got back on the radio to say that Mrs. Gerbers, his former agent's wife, had told him that Chamillus's message had not been received because his Madrid radioman had not stayed on duty as expected. What follows is Pujol's angry and brilliant correspondence with Federico, as well as the steps that followed to convince the Germans to stay focused on Calais, despite the Normandy landings.

"Once this text had been transmitted, GARBO pretended to have received a visit from Mrs. Gerbers, who had informed him, for the first time, about the delay in getting his signals acknowledged the previous morning. GARBO was suitably indignant, and his tone changed from self-congratulation to simulated outrage: 'On handing over today's messages, ALMURA (the Madrid radio operator) told the widow that he was not able to send the urgent messages until 0800 hours since you had not been listening.

"'This makes me question your seriousness and your sense of responsibility. I therefore demand a clarification immediately as to what has occurred. If what I suspect is the case and ALMURA has failed in his duties, then I am absolutely decided in this event to abandon the radio service until I can find some other solution. I am very disgusted; in this struggle for life or death, I cannot accept excuses or negligence. I cannot swallow the idea of endangering the service without any benefit. Were it not for my ideals and faith I would abandon this work as having proved myself a failure! I write these messages to send this very night though my tiredness and exhaustion, due to the excessive work I have had, has completely broken me.'"[10]

In response to this heated message, Federico replied in a very contrite tone attempting to explain why Madrid may have been off duty. Then, rather than blame Pujol's network for not getting information on the invasion to Madrid sooner, he assured them of their competence.

"'I wish to stress in the clearest terms that your work over the last few weeks has made it possible for our command to be completely forewarned and prepared, and the message of CHAMILLUS would have influenced but little had it arrived three or four hours earlier. *Thus I reiterate to you, as responsible chief of the service, and to all your collaborators, our total recognition of your perfect and cherished work, and I beg of you to continue with us in the supreme and decisive hours of the struggle for the future of Europe.*'"[11]

With the Abwehr suitably chastened (not wanting it discovered by the German high command that they'd missed an early warning of the Normandy invasion because their radio operator was tired), they were now ready to take whatever Pujol sent them. It was finally time to set the trap that Operation Garbo had been preparing since the earliest days of the war. Pujol sent the longest message of his career, outlining the reason why his "intelligence" still suggested that the main blow was yet to come from Dover to Calais. Juan Pujol's message and its impact on the German high command are best expressed in his memoir coauthored with Nigel West:

"GARBO was finally ready to start sending at seven minutes past midnight, and the resulting message was sent by Charles Haines for the next 122 minutes. The transmission was easily GARBO's longest and by far his most important, for it encapsulated the entire FORTITUDE deception:

"'From the reports mentioned, it is perfectly clear that the present attack is a large-scale operation but diversionary in character, for the purpose of establishing a strong bridgehead in order to draw the maximum of our reserves to the area of operation and to retain them there so as to be able to strike a blow somewhere else with ensured success.

"'I never like to give my opinions unless I have strong reasons to justify my assurances, but the fact that these concentrations, which are in the east and south-east of the island, are now inactive means that they must be held in reserve to be employed in the other large-scale operations.

"'The constant aerial bombardments which the area of the Pas-de-Calais has suffered and the strategic disposition of these forces give reason to suspect an attack in that region of France which, at the same time, offers the shortest route for the final objective of their illusions, which is to say, Berlin. This advance could be covered by a constant hammering from the air since the bases would be near the field of battle and they would come in behind our forces which are fighting at the present moment with the enemy disembarked in the west of France.

"'From agent J(5) I learned yesterday that there were seventy-five divisions in this country before the present assault commenced. Supposing they should use a maximum of twenty to twenty-five divisions with which to attempt a second blow.

"'I trust you will submit urgently all these reports and studies to our high command, since moments may be decisive in these times and before taking a false step, through lack of knowledge of the necessary facts, they should have in their possession all the present information which I transmit with my opinion, which is based on the belief that the whole of the present attack is set as a trap for the enemy to make us move all our reserves in a hurried strategical disposition which we would later regret.'

"This single message is of extraordinary historic significance, and the decrypters watched its progress through the enemy's military intelligence structure.

"From Madrid it was relayed to Berlin and then delivered to Hitler's headquarters at Berchtesgaden, where it was received by Colonel Friedrich-Adolf Krummacher, the head of the Wehrmacht High Command's intelligence branch.

"By that time it had been edited several times and code names had been slightly corrupted in the process, but it is entirely recognizable when compared to MI5's original version, and the central theme remained intact: *After personal consultation on 8 June in London with my agents JONNY, DICK and DORICK, whose reports were sent today, I am of the opinion, in view of the strong troop concentrations in south-eastern and eastern England, which are not taking part in the present operations, that these operations are a diversionary maneuver designed to draw off enemy reserves in order then to make a decisive attack in another place. In view of the continued air attacks on the concentration area mentioned, which is a strategically favourable position for this, it may very probably take place in the Pas-de-Calais area, particularly since in such an attack the proximity of air bases will facilitate the operation by providing continued strong air support.'*

"After the war the actual document summarizing GARBO's opinion was recovered intact, and a further assessment had been added by the German High Command: 'The report is credible. The reports received in the last week from the ARABEL [Pujol] undertaking have been confirmed almost without exception and are to be described as especially valuable. The main line of investigation in future is to be the enemy group of forces in south-eastern and eastern England.'

"When Krummacher received the summary he underlined the sentence characterizing the Normandy landings as 'diversionary in nature' and added the written comment: *'Confirms the view already held by us that a further attack is to be expected in another place (Belgium?)'*

"Before being handed to Hitler, this paper was passed to Field Marshal Jodl, who initialed it and underscored the words 'south-eastern and eastern England.' Evidently, GARBO's poison had proved particularly efficacious on him.

"It was later established that this single message had a devastating effect on the German high command and led to the cancellation of a major armoured counter-attack in Normandy, using seasoned units from the Pas-de-Calais area. Instead, the troops en route were ordered to return to their bases. The much-feared armoured thrust simply never materialized, and credit for this coup can be given to GARBO."[12]

And thus it was that after nearly five years of living in an imaginary world of spies and spying, Operation Garbo successfully averted a major German counterattack on the Allied troops landing in Normandy.

OPERATION GARBO—THE AFTERMATH

In the weeks that followed the invasion, Operation Garbo continued on. To keep the rumor of a major advance against Calais alive, even as nearly a million Allied troops were pouring into Normandy, Pujol's group first falsely reported that imaginary units held in reserve in the north for an invasion of Norway were seen to be moving to southeast England. He indicated to Federico that he believed this confirmed that Norway was off the table, but that an attack on the Pas-de-Calais was still imminent. His acknowledgment was accepted.

But then the Germans started asking questions that were so specific in nature that it would require Pujol to report real intelligence that *would* be used against the Allies. It was time to dial down the temperature. The way that Tommy Harris decided to do that was to have Pujol pretend to start carrying out the Abwehr's request, only to have him disappear. One of his agents then reported to Madrid that Pujol had been arrested by the British, and that it looked like they were closing in on the rest of them. The Abwehr held their breath. Finally, after a suitable absence, Pujol transmitted again that he was out of jail, but that it had been a near thing. He relocated and started broadcasting again—but no longer under the obligation to betray the truth that the Germans had been seeking.

In late 1944 two remarkable things happened. Garbo was notified that he was to receive the Iron Cross from Germany for his heroic efforts on their behalf. Second, he was also nominated and accepted to receive membership in the Order of the British Empire (OBE). Of course, the presentation of these awards had to remain secret, so the Iron Cross was sent to England by diplomatic carrier. He received the OBE in person from Sir David Petrie in a small celebration at which all senior officers in MI5 who had clearance to know of Operation Garbo were in attendance. Pujol was a double-decorated double-agent!

He continued to broadcast until nearly the end of the war. His greatest value to the Allies after Normandy was through the reverse telescope, in which the specific requests from Germany indicated what was on their mind and where their concerns were. As the noose tightened around Nazi Germany, Pujol and the Abwehr decided that for his safety he should go into hiding. Prior to doing so, Federico sent him a remarkable message showing how completely the Abwehr had been taken in by his deceptions:

"'I should like to be a writer in order that I should have facility to find the words which might fully give you to understand the high esteem which we all have for you and the desire we and our headquarters have to collaborate with you.

"'We have, in your personality, your character, your valour, all these virtues which become a gentleman. I hope, nevertheless, that from what I have written to you, you will have been able to feel that which perhaps through lack of ability to express myself in the written word I have been unable to impress adequately.

"'We here, in the very small circle of colleagues who know your story and that of your organization, talk so often about you that it often seems as if we were living the incidents which you relate to us, and we most certainly share, to the full, your worries.'"[13]

At the end of the war Operation Garbo was classified as "Most Secret" and word of it was never made public until more than fifty years later. Juan Pujol and his family returned to Madrid briefly, but Pujol soon became worried that overzealous former Nazis might seek revenge on him, or his wife and children, if they discovered that he had been a double agent. He decided to move to Venezuela to live out the rest of his life. Before leaving, he arranged to meet with Federico one last time. His Abwehr contact was sentimental, decrying the great opportunity that was lost to Europe and the world in Germany's defeat. He also reiterated his great appreciation for the work Pujol had done on behalf of the Third Reich, never suspecting for a moment that he had been duped from the very beginning.

Pujol and his story would likely have remained untold had it not been for the interest showed by Nigel West, a journalist and author, who had been tantalized by a brief conversation with a former MI5 agent about a Spaniard who had helped in the war. He decided to track down this individual, and through a series of small clues eventually teased out that a man by the name of Pujol or Garcia had somehow been connected to the intelligence service. From that he tracked Juan Pujol down and reached out to him about the story. Deciding that after fifty years it was finally safe to come out of the shadows, Pujol admitted that he was Agent Garbo. Nigel West helped him write and publish his story. As the truth became known, people wanted to celebrate Pujol-Garcia's accomplishments. This led to a series of events to bring his story to light, culminating in a visit to England's Buckingham Palace.

It is appropriate to allow Juan Pujol Garcia to have the last word in this remarkable story:

"For the next thirty-six years I lived peacefully in Venezuela; it was a quiet time for me, for my life of action, of fighting for freedom, for my ideals, was over. Then in 1984, when I was least expecting it, Nigel West broke the cover that I had so successfully maintained and, through painstaking research and careful investigation, tracked me down.

"A few days before the fortieth anniversary of the D-Day landings, he called on the telephone from London. He said how glad he was to be able to talk to the person whom everyone had thought to be dead. Even though I wanted to forget all about the war, he was so insistent that I relented; he persuaded me that I would enjoy seeing old colleagues again and I was flattered at the thought of being introduced to HRH the Duke of Edinburgh, who, he said, was very keen to meet me.

"So many promises and offers were made that I agreed to think it over. After I was sure that all my German contacts had either disappeared or died, I decided that the time had come for my family to learn about my past, to hear about that part of my life which I had concealed from them up until now for security reasons.

"And so I returned to London to receive personal thanks from the Duke of Edinburgh (Prince Philip, husband of Queen Elizabeth II) at Buckingham Palace, my acknowledgment from the people of Britain of all that I had done to help them retain their democracy and their freedom, and an example of their gratitude for backing their courageous fight against the Nazis. For it was their resolute stand and their humane conduct which had driven me all those years ago to offer to help, so that we could work hand in hand for victory in the battle of good against evil.

"But my main pride and satisfaction, now I look back, has been the knowledge that I contributed to the reduction of casualties among the thousands—the tens of thousands—of servicemen fighting to hold the Normandy beachheads. Many, many more would have perished had our plan failed and the Germans counter-attacked in force."[14]

CHAPTER 5

CARL LUTZ SAVES 72,000 JEWISH LIVES

INTRODUCTION

Starting on March 19, 1944, a series of cudgel blows prepared unsuspecting Hungarian Jewry for its extinction:

1. Arrest of all the moderate politicians who had tried to extricate Hungary from its fatal alliance with Nazi Germany and who had protected the Jews
2. Required wearing of the yellow star (Jews could thus be easily recognized, molested in public, and arrested without warrant)
3. Confiscation of apartments and housing, officially in favor of "Christians" who had lost their homes during Allied air raids
4. Prohibition of travel, no ownership of telephones or radios, suspension of mail service
5. Confiscation of real estate

6. Loss of jobs in industry, banking, commerce, social
   services, and state offices
7. Loss of movable property, bank accounts, jewelry, etc.
8. House arrest for all Jews, except for two hours each
   day to make purchases, etc.

From one moment to the next, Hungarian Jews not only
became paupers—they were made beggars.[1]

Although Hungary had been a member of the Axis powers from
1940, fighting alongside the Nazis in Yugoslavia and in the Soviet
Union, the Hungarian Jewish population had been spared the worst
of the anti-Jewish pogroms of other Axis countries, including the
death camps in Germany. But that changed in early 1944 when the
Hungarian regent, Admiral Miklos Horthy, entered into secret negotiations with the United States and Great Britain to sign an armistice that would end Hungary's alliance with Germany and take
its troops out of the war. Word of the negotiations leaked to the
Germans, who sent troops to occupy Hungary.

Toward the end of the year, when the Soviet Union threatened
to invade Hungary, Horthy again acted against Germany's interests
by signing an armistice with the USSR. The outraged Germans responded by kidnapping Horthy's son and holding him hostage until
Horthy revoked the armistice. He was then deposed and replaced by
a pro-Nazi Hungarian fascist leader, Ferenc Szalasi, who agreed to
lead the country under the direction of Berlin.

Thus it was that in March 1944 the Jewish population of
Hungary lost all their civil rights, including protection from deportation to the Auschwitz death camp in German-occupied Poland,
where 437,000 Hungarian Jews were gassed to death and cremated.
They were betrayed by the country where they had lived side by
side with Christians for nearly 2,000 years. Like Jews in other Axis
countries, they too had lived in fear of the rumors of what was happening in the concentration camps of Germany, but had comforted

themselves with the thought that "it will never happen here" because of their faith in the long-established "Jewish-Christian symbiosis" that had allowed Hungary's Jews to actively participate in the economic success of the country. But in the face of German ultimatums for Hungary to resolve the "Jewish question," the symbiosis proved itself a mirage and nearly eighty percent of Hungary's Jews lost their lives before the end of the war.

A notable exception to this brutal surrender to Nazi anti-Semitism was found at the Swiss legation in Budapest where the Swiss minister, Maximillian Jaeger, empowered his vice-consul, Carl Lutz, to extend Swiss protection to tens of thousands of Hungarian Jews who desperately sought his help in avoiding extradition to Auschwitz. Lutz is credited with personally saving the lives of up to 72,000 Jews. He and other courageous diplomats from neutral countries saved nearly half the Jewish population of Budapest. In leading these efforts, Carl Lutz put himself at odds with both the puppet government of Hungary and with the brutal and desperate Third Reich in Berlin.

Lutz's is a story of personal courage and compassion. Yet immediately after the war he was censured by the Swiss diplomatic service for overreaching his authority by using his diplomatic credentials to protect the Jews. After the great danger he had placed himself in, almost no one knew of his deeds or thanked him. But Jewish people all around the world knew of Carl Lutz, and they revered him. Finally, in 1957, the Swiss Federal Assembly formally recognized his humanitarian achievements in the Second World War. In 1965 he was named to the list of "Righteous among the Nations" by Yad Vashem, Israel's Holocaust Remembrance Authority. Other awards followed, including one from the country of his former enemies, the Cross of Honor–Order of Merit of the Federal Republic of Germany.

Reading of Lutz's courage while under constant pressure leaves the reader breathless as time after time he stood directly between a powerless Jew and the street gangs and military troops that occupied Budapest in the last desperate days of the war, using both his body and his words as a shield against the oppressor. Yet he never thought himself a hero.

CARL LUTZ

Carl Lutz was born in the mountains of Walzenhausen, Switzerland, on March 30, 1895. He was the ninth child in his family. His father owned a sandstone quarry and his mother was a Methodist Sunday School teacher. Although she was highly religious, it was in a practical sense: "Reflecting on the poverty of the Appenzell hill country, she admonished her children that it was more important to help those in need than to always run to prayer meetings."[2] His mother's religious devotion influenced Lutz for the rest of his life, including his time as the Swiss consul in Budapest helping the Jews.

After his father died when Carl was fourteen, Lutz struggled with school, mostly because he had progressed beyond what the small local school could offer him. And he needed to help his family financially, so he apprenticed at a nearby textile mill. At age eighteen he decided to immigrate to America, where he hoped to find more career opportunities. He was initially disappointed, finding a low-paying clerk job in a factory in Illinois. When America was drawn into World War I in 1917 he was determined not to go to war, so he spent three months in hiding, moving between Tennessee, Kentucky, Louisiana, and Oklahoma to avoid the draft. He finally emerged from this solitude in 1918 and enrolled in the Methodist-owned Western Wesleyan College in Missouri. His time in hiding left a lasting impression. Reflecting on it later, he wrote, "When I looked into the faces of the Budapest Jews nearly thirty years later, I knew what it was like to be trapped."[3]

Two years later Carl Lutz found his life's calling—he left

Western Wesleyan College and went to Washington, DC, to work as a staff member at the Swiss legation. Here he was finally challenged both intellectually and socially. He flourished in the complicated political atmosphere of the capital city of the United States. He also enrolled in part-time studies at the prestigious George Washington University, specializing in diplomacy, and graduated in 1924. The Swiss minister to the United States recognized Lutz's talent and recommended him to the diplomatic service in Bern. Traveling back to Switzerland, he passed his examinations and was accepted into the service. He asked for an assignment in Europe but was sent back to the United States for another ten years. He got to know America very well, working in Washington, New York, Philadelphia, and St. Louis.

It was in St. Louis that he met a young woman, Gertrude Fankhauser, who breached the romantic rectitude of the thirty-nine-year-old bachelor. He was smitten. She was vivacious and charming, full of energy and life. At first, she was reluctant to accept his romantic overtures, but he was, if nothing else, persistent, and determined. Eventually Gertrude accepted his proposal of marriage, and after some additional hesitation on her part, they returned to Switzerland in January 1935.

Once again, Lutz had asked for reassignment to Europe to be closer to their families, but at the very last moment—literally on the day of his marriage—the Swiss foreign ministry decided to send him to Jaffa in Palestine in response to a diplomatic emergency instead of to London as planned. So, after exchanging their vows, the newlyweds boarded a train for Venice and then a steamship to the Middle East.

"Curiously, shortly before they parted at the end of the wedding reception, his mother, Ursula, slipped a piece of paper into her son's hand. She was now in her eighties, and her handwriting was becoming shaky. She had written a passage from the prophet Isaiah: 'And he shall be a father to the inhabitants of Jerusalem and to the house of Judah.' Perhaps his mother had a presentiment."[4]

Whether his mother was prophetic or not, it was in Palestine that Lutz came to appreciate the Jews and to feel for the persecution they faced all over the world. For example, as anti-Semitism increased throughout Europe, many Jewish people applied to the British for immigration to Palestine. This enraged the Palestinians who already occupied the area and who viewed the Jews as their historic enemies of more than 3,000 years, extending all the way back to the prophet Abraham. Frequent clashes between the Jews and Arabs spilled violence onto the streets. One particularly disturbing event changed Carl and Gertrude forever when they witnessed a mob of Palestinians surround a lone Jewish man and lynch him in broad daylight on the street below their hotel window. Because they were often mistaken for Jews, and thus at risk of being killed themselves if they intervened, they watched helplessly from the window as the execution took place.

For their part, the British were not sure how to keep the peace. As increasing numbers of Jews applied for asylum in their historic homeland, the Palestinians became ever more agitated and angrier. Finally, the British set a cap on Jewish immigration of just 75,000 people to take place over the five-year period from 1939 through 1944. After that, no more Jews would be allowed into Palestine without local consent. With millions of lives in danger in Nazi-occupied territories, this was a paltry figure. Still, it did offer hope to some and the Jewish Agency for Palestine was given authority to issue "Palestine certificates" that allowed up to 75,000 European Jews, a majority being women and children, to legally immigrate to Palestine. Remarkably, even during the Jewish pogroms in the Axis countries, most governments honored these certificates. It was a beginning.

On September 1, 1939, just a month before Germany invaded

Poland, the Nazi government in Berlin asked Switzerland to assume responsibility for its operations in Palestine as Germany prepared for war. Carl Lutz was promoted to vice-consul and soon was responsible for the safety and welfare of thousands of German embassy and consulate employees in Jaffa, as well as for overseeing more than 70,000 German Jews who were then in the Holy Land. It was an exhausting responsibility that he handled with dignity and patience. The Germans expressed their appreciation for his outstanding work on their behalf.

In this way he had become an expert in understanding the intricacies and perils of Jewish affairs. Lutz returned to Switzerland in 1940 and in January 1942 Carl was assigned to Budapest where, with the able support of Gertrude, he was about to meet his destiny.

BUDAPEST IN WORLD WAR II

When war broke out between the United States and Germany in December 1941, the Americans were obliged to withdraw their legation in Budapest and to abandon their spacious six-story building in the main center of Pest at Freedom Square.[5] They asked the Swiss legation to take up residence and oversee America's diplomatic interests in their absence. Vice-consul Lutz was ideally suited to this assignment given his twenty years of service in the United States. His primary offices were moved to this new building, away from the main Swiss diplomatic mission led by Minister Jaeger. He and Gertrude lived in the former British Embassy in Buda, west of the Danube River. The former American legation building was to become Lutz's command center for conducting all the ordinary affairs of the Swiss legation, as well as the absentee administration of British and American interests in Hungary. From 1942 to 1944 these were his primary activities. Then Germany occupied Hungary, and his attention turned to the new threat posed to the Budapest Jews.

As the new German foreign minister, Edmund Veesenmayer,

and SS *Obersturmbannführer* [the SS equivalent of lieutenant colonel] Adolf Eichmann began to assert their control over the puppet government of Hungary, they became Lutz's chief foils in the battle for control over the fate of the Jews.

What Carl and Gertrude Lutz did not know, even as late in the war as 1944, was the extent of Germany's holocaust against Jews in all their other occupied territories. By 1944 it is likely that more than five million Jews had been murdered. But Hungary had not yet participated in sending Jews to the death camps. Lutz was at a disadvantage when he was introduced to Eichmann, whom Veesenmayer had said was a "transportation specialist" who could maybe help Lutz with his request to honor the previously approved transfer of 8,000 Jewish children to Palestine.

In truth, Eichmann was in Hungary to organize death trains to Auschwitz with the goal of killing all of Hungary's nearly 800,000 Jews. In early 1944, it was becoming clear that Germany was in danger of losing the war, so the urgency of implementing this "final solution" was increasing each day.

The first diplomatic dance between Lutz and Eichmann occurred over Lutz's request for help with the 8,000 children who held Palestine certificates that were in good order. Lutz reminded Eichmann that these orders had always been honored by all the countries where they were legitimately held, and now Germany could assist in processing them. Eichmann was solicitous, saying that he would be pleased to help the vice-consul, but that as an ordinary soldier he had to receive written authority from SS headquarters in Berlin. When Lutz asked if he would cable Berlin for an answer, Eichmann replied that it was hardly the place of a subordinate to suggest a course of action to a superior officer. Lutz left the meeting frustrated. For his part, Eichmann recognized that Lutz was likely to work against his interests, so he advanced the timetable for rounding up Hungarian Jews to send to Auschwitz.

THE AUSCHWITZ-BUCHENWALD
CONCENTRATION (DEATH) CAMP

After exiting the trains, the prisoners were taken to "a large 'reception hall,' which [was] arranged so as to give the impression of the antechamber of a bathing establishment. It [held] 2,000 people and apparently there [was] a similar waiting room on the floor below. From there a door and a few steps [led] down into the very long and narrow gas chamber. The walls of this chamber [were] camouflaged with simulated entries to shower rooms in order to mislead the victims. This roof [was] fitted with three traps which [could] be hermetically closed from the outside. A track [led] from the gas chamber to the furnace room.

"The gassing [took] place as follows: the unfortunate victims [were] brought into hall (B) where they [were] told to undress. To complete the fiction that they [were] going to bathe, each person [received] a small towel and a small piece of soap issued by two men clad in white coats. They [were] then crowded into the gas chamber (C) in such numbers there [was], of course, only standing room. To compress this crowd into the narrow space, shots [were] often fired to induce those already at the far end to huddle still closer together.

"When everybody [was] inside, the heavy doors [were] closed. Then there [was] a short pause, presumably to allow the room temperature to rise to a certain level, after which SS men with gas masks [climbed] on the roof, [opened] the traps, and [shook] down a preparation in powder form out of tin cans labeled 'CYKLON' and 'For use against vermin,' which [was] manufactured by a Hamburg concern. It is presumed that this [was] a 'cyanide' mixture of some sort which turns into gas at a certain temperature. *After three minutes everyone in the chamber [was] dead.* No one is known to have survived this ordeal, although it was not uncommon to discover signs of life after the primitive measures employed in the Birch Wood. The chamber [was] then opened, aired, and the 'special squad' [carted] the bodies on flat trucks to the furnace rooms where the burning [took] place."[6]

This was the fate that awaited the Hungarian Jews, though the Germans carefully concealed the truth while assembling and transporting them to Auschwitz. This quote comes from a document known as the "Auschwitz Protocols" and was written by two Jewish prisoners, Rudolf Vrba and Alfred Wetzler, who managed to escape from the camp. They wrote the protocols and then delivered them to Jewish authorities in Budapest. It should have set off immediate alarms and sent hundreds of thousands into hiding. But many of the Jewish leaders in Hungary found it too incredible to believe, so it was not made known to the general Jewish population. Ultimately, a copy was delivered to Carl Lutz who was furious that he had not received a copy earlier, and who then realized the malevolent nature of the German monster that he was up against.

In preparing to write his book *Dangerous Diplomacy*, author Theo Tschuy researched how Adolf Eichmann implemented Hitler's "final solution" in Hungary. It is a chilling tale that is necessary to read to fully appreciate the mission that Carl Lutz undertook for himself.

"In region after region the SS, the Hungarian gendarmes, aided by local political authorities, transmitted their orders to the condemned Jews through the local Jewish councils to turn over their last belongings, leave their homes, and march to their assembly points. They were told that they would be resettled 'in a nice place,' where all their needs would be met. If his own religious authorities said so, it must be true, the ordinary Jew felt. Without fuss the victims were assembled in makeshift concentration camps, which were usually located in abandoned factories or brickyards, away from population centers, but conveniently close to railway yards. Surprised as they may have been, the members of the local Jewish councils were ordered to join the others in the queue.

"The 'final solution' could succeed only if credulity and secrecy were maintained.

"When the marchers were herded together at the assembly points, often under great brutality, it would dawn on even the least informed that they and the Jewish councils had been duped and that a terrible fate awaited them. But even then, up to the very end, few could imagine what a death camp was like. Such a monstrosity was beyond human comprehension.

"If someone objected to having to leave home or if there was resistance, an SS or gendarmerie officer would shoot him or her in the neck in sight of everyone else. The rest would not rebel.

"News of the deportations was nevertheless often leaked out to the local Christian populations, who could guess what was happening to the Jews. Sometimes people would come out of their houses and watch the marching columns. These Jews were, after all, their neighbors, bakers, storekeepers, tailors, or innkeepers. They had played together with them as children and had often remained on friendly terms with them, despite anti-Semitism and name-calling. *If individual Christian Hungarians protested, as did happen on occasion, the gendarmes seized them and deported them along with the Jews.* The gendarmes even mistreated those Christians whom they caught with tears running down their cheeks.

"For days and often weeks on end the deportees were exposed in the makeshift camps to sunshine and rain, heat and cold, with few latrines and barely any food available. They endured these brutal conditions until the day the cattle wagons and the train engines pulled up and [the] unfortunates were pushed through the narrow doors without mercy.

"The first train left Hungary for Auschwitz on May 15, 1944. It arrived two days later, on the 17th. It was composed of over forty sealed cattle wagons with 100 persons in each. On a special railway track these 4,000 human beings stopped directly in front of the gas chambers at Auschwitz-Birkenau. They were gassed and burned immediately, except for seventeen men who—by orders of Dr. Mengele—were temporarily allowed to stay alive in order to do the 'cleaning up' of the empty wagons.

"On the next day, May 18, another deportation train arrived with 4,000 persons aboard. This time twenty women were allowed to stay alive and were brought to the barracks. *During the first four days 16,000 Hungarian Jews were killed.* On May 21, no less than three trains arrived, carrying 12,000 people, of whom only eleven men and women were left alive. All the rest lost their lives immediately upon arrival. During the same day deportation trains also arrived from Holland and Belgium. One of these was filled with Gypsies (the Roma) of whom Nazi Germany murdered several hundreds of thousands. Never before had the death camp of Auschwitz-Birkenau gone into such high gear.

"Each day Minister Veesenmayer cabled the numbers of those who had been sent to 'labor service.' He mentioned Auschwitz as the destination point."[7]

So even while losing ground in their war against the Allies, the Nazi regime kept the ovens at their six main killing camps busy night and day burning the bodies of the Jewish people they had kidnapped and killed.

FRIENDS AND FOES

Everywhere he traveled in and around Buda and Pest, Carl Lutz was besieged by frightened Jews who appealed to him for protection. In a strictly legal and diplomatic sense he should not have become involved—after all, a foreign power does not have the authority to interfere with the internal affairs of a host country. But Lutz refused to stand aside as the horror of the holocaust unfolded. So he came up with innovative strategies to offer protection to the local Jews.

Here is his firsthand account of just one of hundreds of incidents from his time in Budapest:

"Five thousand of these unhappy people were standing in line, freezing, shaking, hungry, with tiny packs on their shoulders, stretching their letters out towards me. Never, never shall I forget those despairing horror-stricken faces. Again, and again the police had to intervene to prevent my clothes being torn from my back. For these people it was the last glimmer of hope; for us, this screening was the worst form of spiritual torture. We saw the people being lashed with dog-whips and lying in the slime and mud with bloody faces. Whenever we tried to help them, we, in our turn, were threatened with rifles. Whenever possible I would drive alongside these people on their way to the concentration camps to try and show them that there was still hope, until my way was blocked by the guards."[8]

Just what could Carl Lutz do to help the Jewish people in Budapest? He developed four strategies:

First, he issued Swiss *Schutzbriefes* to as many Jews as possible. A Schutzbriefe was a diplomatic protective order issued to an individual indicating that he or she was under the protection of a foreign government and requesting all national and local authorities to assist in keeping that person safe. Prior to the Nazi occupation in 1944, the government of Hungary had given Lutz authority to issue 8,000 of these protective orders to Jewish children who were eligible to immigrate to Palestine. Lutz soon realized that this would never be sufficient, so ultimately he issued many more—all numbered between 1 and 8,000. Since the people who held these protective orders were scattered about, it was almost impossible for the Nazis or local authorities to ever find two with the same number at the same time.

When challenged on issuing more orders than were authorized, Lutz asserted that he had been given authority to issue 8,000 orders to *families*, since it made no sense to send minor children alone. For more than two years Lutz and the people he protected were challenged by the Germans and unfriendly Hungarian officials, but the Schutzbriefes were largely honored, even though they were resented.

Second, Lutz allowed a limited number of Jewish people to take up residence in the American legation building, which was considered foreign soil under international law. Thus, once a person moved onto the compound, it was as if he or she were no longer in Hungary, but were protected under Swiss law. Hundreds of Jewish lives were saved by this kindness.

Third, in a daringly bold diplomatic maneuver, Lutz extended extraterritorial status to seventy-two other residential buildings in Pest, allowing their Jewish residents to live under Swiss protection. This was bitterly resented by Eichmann and his Hungarian counterparts, but they feared alienating Switzerland, through which arms were shipped to Germany. Each time they tried to counter Lutz's strategy he found new ways to maintain his protection over these apartment buildings.

Fourth, to extend his influence, Vice-consul Lutz started meeting with other delegations from neutral countries to assist in his efforts. This group undertook several initiatives, including writing a letter of protest to the Hungarian government about their support for the extermination of the Jews, requesting that they prohibit future transport to German-occupied Poland. Since Nuncio Angelo Rotta (an ambassador for the Vatican) signed this letter, it carried extra weight with believing Catholics in the government. In response the government did cancel Eichmann's trains for a few months.

The neutral nations also adopted Lutz's tactic of inviting Jews into their compounds and extending extraterritorial status to other buildings. The Swedish legation was particularly active in this regard, and was led by the courageous and energetic Raoul Wallenberg, also later named to the "Righteous Among the Nations" list of Israel's heroes. Wallenberg extended Swedish protection to an additional thirty-two safe houses.

Four groups in Hungary caused Vice-consul Lutz and his allies trouble; three in direct opposition and one whose indifference still hindered their work.

The first were the Nazi occupying forces. Minister Veesenmayer and Lieutenant Colonel Eichmann were specifically tasked with deporting *all* Hungarian Jews to Auschwitz to be murdered in the gas chambers. They were under constant pressure from Berlin to step up their efforts, even as thousands of Jews were being shipped in railroad cattle cars each day. Lutz was an impediment to their efforts, and they made appeals and demands to the Hungarian government to press for his recall to Switzerland. He was in constant danger of being declared persona non grata by the Hungarian government, which would have forced him to return to Switzerland.

The second group consisted of anti-Semitic Hungarians both within the government and within the neighborhoods. By taking Jewish homes, apartments, and possessions and giving them to their Christian neighbors, the Hungarian government made accomplices out of many ordinary Hungarians who then betrayed their former Jewish neighbors, including those who were in hiding. Some Hungarian citizens accosted Jews wearing the yellow Star of David on the streets, and they both tacitly and explicitly supported the idea of a Jewish-free Hungary, which empowered the Germans to continue the deportations. Not a few Hungarian gendarmes also assisted in concentrating Jews in camps all across Hungary prior to being forced to board the death trains.

Most Hungarian government leaders were either complicit in aiding in these efforts or they were willing to turn a blind eye to what was happening so that the Nazis could move forward unimpeded. Lutz and his supporters had to constantly remind these officials that the eyes of the world were on them and that they would one day be judged for their complicity, given that it was now clear that Germany was destined to lose the war with the Allies. It was only because of those threats that Hungarian government officials continued to honor the Schutzbriefes and to allow Lutz to remain in the country.

The third group were Hungarian gangs, including the Arrow Cross, a paramilitary group that ultimately assumed government control of much of Pest when the Soviet army bombarded the city, and the Nyilas, roving gangs of young men who beat up people on the street, executed Jews in broad daylight, and who stole and plundered as the city's social structures collapsed under the weight of the Soviet invasion. These groups were the most dangerous of all to Lutz and other neutral country diplomats' personal safety, since they were uneducated in diplomatic protocols. On more than one occasion they threatened to shoot Lutz if he failed to step aside from Jews they wanted to massacre. But he always stood his ground, intimidating them by his knowledge of international law and by his sheer courage in stepping between the gangs and the Jews he was resolved to protect.

The fourth group who impeded Lutz were international diplomats who were indifferent to the plight of the Jews. This was a large group, including many in the Swiss Foreign Ministry in Bern who were frustrated by Lutz's aggressive actions in Hungary. But it did not stop in Switzerland; England often expressed frustration that Lutz was overstepping his bounds, and American military leaders would not divert any resources to bomb the concentration camps. All of this changed briefly when the Auschwitz Protocols were released to the world, but the outrage quickly subsided and Carl Lutz, Raoul Wallenberg, and others were again left on their own.

Fortunately, Lutz's boss, Swiss minister Maximillian Jaegar, was both independently wealthy (so not intimidated by officials in Bern) and active in his support for Lutz's efforts. Later, after Jaegar was recalled to Bern, in part because of his support for the Jews, his successor Harald Feller also supported Lutz.

Thus, for nearly two years, Lutz placed his life on the line to oppose these cruel forces and to use ever more desperate measures to save as many people as he possibly could. Even so, he could not save everyone—not even a majority—and in his daily automobile drives out into the city he had to witness street executions, beatings, and looting of people who were guilty of nothing more than having been born a Jew.

A BRIEF REPRIEVE—GEORGE MANDEL-MANTELLO

In June 1944, a Hungarian-born Jewish diplomat named George Mandel-Mantello, working at the Salvadoran embassy in Bern and thus safe from deportation to Germany, managed to buy the Jews of his homeland a much needed but temporary reprieve from deportation. His was a story of a chance meeting that had a profound impact on world opinion. Just how did a Hungarian Jew come to be working at the Salvadoran embassy in Bern, Switzerland, at a crucial moment in world history? It turns out that in the late 1930s Mantello had been a textile manufacturer in Bucharest, Romania, where he happened to meet the Salvadoran consul to Romania, Jose Arturo Castellanos. They became friends.

When the Nazis came to power not long after that, Mantello escaped to Switzerland before the border was closed to Jews. It was natural that he sought out his friend (who had been reassigned to the Salvadoran embassy in Bern) for a job. Mantello was appointed first secretary. He was in this position when the Auschwitz Protocols were smuggled into Switzerland.

Outraged, he wondered why the world did not rise in indignation. The reason was that no one in authority was willing to print and distribute the documents, fearing it would upset the delicate international trade regimes with the Germans. So Mantello went to work on his own. Printing over 1,000 copies, he sent the Protocols to newspapers and governments all around the world. When word of the outrages at Auschwitz were finally released to the public, a furor arose that swept aside diplomatic skittishness. This was particularly true when the Pope expressed his outrage at this new information about the subhuman treatment of the Jews. In America, President Franklin Roosevelt sent a furious demand to the government of Hungary, delivered through vice-consul Carl Lutz, insisting that they order an immediate cessation of all deportations to Germany, with the threat that there would be criminal prosecutions after the war if his demands were not met. To prove the point, he ordered American aircraft to bomb military facilities in Budapest as a show of his anger. British Prime Minister Winston Churchill wrote of the Protocols, "There is no doubt that this persecution of Jews in Hungary and their expulsion from enemy territory is probably the greatest and most horrible crime ever committed in the whole history of the world."[9]

All of this had the immediate effect of causing the Horthy government in Hungary to order a cease-and-desist order to Veesenmayer and Eichmann, and for the moment the trains stopped running. Germany denied that the Auschwitz Protocols were true—suggesting that they were simply faked information to embarrass Germany. But the Nazis did not resist the Hungarian order to stop the trains. What was unknown to anyone in the world but to the three people directly involved was that it was Lutz who had passed the Protocols to a Jewish minister in Budapest who then used the Swiss diplomatic pouch to send them to Switzerland. If authorities in the Foreign Ministry learned of Lutz's role in the release, it would have resulted in his recall to Bern. Fortunately, Mantello suggested that the Protocols had come to him from Istanbul to protect the people involved.

Two positive things resulted from Montello's release of the

Protocols: First, the secret of the Nazi death camps was finally out in the open, with firsthand accounts of their vicious, inhuman operations made public across the globe. Second, many thousands of lives were saved when Hungary canceled deportations for two months since the Germans ultimately ran out of time.

But from a moral point of view, even the release of the Protocols had failed to dissuade anti-Semites from carrying forward with their plans to eliminate the Jews. It simply stalled them for a period. For, in time, as world attention turned back to the war, the Germans insisted that a new government be installed in Hungary that would allow them to begin anew. It was not long before the trains were running again.

"THE GREATEST MAN I HAVE EVER MET"

Against thousands of years of history, the eighteen months from when death trains started rolling until the Soviet Union finally liberated the Jews from their oppressors on January 15, 1945, seems like a short moment of time. But when placed in the context of 12,000 Jews *per day* being sent to their death at Auschwitz, every single day counted—even more so as Hungarian society and social order began to fall apart in the last months of 1944 and roving bands of Nyilas and the Arrow Cross started killing Jews openly in Budapest itself.

For eighteen months Lutz and his supporters had to intervene on a daily basis to insist on the sanctity of their safe houses, or to persuade a group of Nyilas that it was in their best interest to leave the Jews alone, or to threaten the leaders of the Arrow Cross that they would be held to account in postwar tribunals for any Jews killed as they asserted that they were the legitimate Hungarian government. They never knew until the very end whether all their efforts would be in vain. It was exhausting and demoralizing, but Lutz forced himself out into the streets every single day to do what he could. Here is one striking example of his courage.

"One scene was related by Geoffrey Tier, the English professor-spy who happened to accompany the consul on several of his dangerous tours. Lutz heard shots coming from the Danube shore, near the House of Parliament. He made Szluha (his driver) speed in that direction. The three men came upon one of the Rivershore executions. When the Packard drove up and braked to a noisy stop, the consul found a Nyilas band, which having completed the execution of a group of Jews, stood by the river shore watching their victims being carried away by the rapidly flowing water. Here and there they shot a bullet after them if they detected signs of life. When Lutz and his companions rushed out of the car, a woman shouted from the water: 'Consul Lutz, Consul Lutz, help me!' She had been shot in the stomach. She pressed one hand on the wound and splashed in the water with the other, trying to stay afloat.

"Lutz knew she would soon lose her strength and drown. The woman managed to swim to the wall where the consul stood. There was a staircase leading into the water, where in more peaceful times small boats were moored. Without a moment's hesitation Lutz went down the staircase. He stood in the water up to his waist, and when the woman came near, he grabbed her. The ice-cold water, which would have frozen her to death within minutes, had an unexpected beneficial effect, in that it luckily closed off the wound.

"With her teeth chattering she tried to explain to the consul that he himself had given her a protective letter. He answered that this was not important now and that she should not talk. Paper or no paper, she was protected by him. With Tier's and Szluha's aid he pulled her out and placed her in the backseat of the Packard. Like a madman Szluha raced off to Freedom Square. Luckily, among the refugees in the basement of the former American legation building there was a Jewish surgeon, who immediately organized a primitive operation room and performed surgery. The woman survived.

"Having observed actions such as these close at hand, Tier's admiration for the consul knew no bounds. Years later, in London, during a talk about Carl Lutz to Swiss students of English, the professor exclaimed glowingly: '*He was the greatest man I have ever met!*'"[10]

More than once, Carl Lutz stepped between a German or a Nyila or a member of the Arrow Cross and the helpless Jew they intended to shoot, placing his life at risk for theirs.

THE SOVIETS ATTACK AND END THE WAR

In the desperate last days of 1944, Adolf Eichmann did everything possible to increase deportations. Eventually, all the trains in Hungary were needed by the Nazi military as they fought a battle to the death with the Soviets, and the death trains came to an end. Eichmann later expressed remorse that he had failed to kill every single Jew in Hungary. Eichmann was tried by a postwar war crimes tribunal and was executed in Jerusalem in 1962 for his crimes against humanity. Carl Lutz said that he often thought of the photo of Eichmann's wife and children that stood behind Eichmann's desk in Budapest and wondered how a man who loved his family could kill, without remorse, more than half a million people in the most barbarous way imaginable.

More than 185,000 German soldiers were sent to Hungary to resist the Soviet advance. As the overwhelming superior forces of the Soviet army moved against them, their leaders petitioned Adolf Hitler for permission to surrender. He issued orders to fight to the last man. Just 785 survived.

After the Nazis failed in Budapest, the Nyilas and Arrow Cross dominated the streets. Lutz found himself isolated in Buda because the Soviets had destroyed all the bridges across the Danube to Pest. Fortunately, he had installed two very capable assistants in Pest, who continued his fight on behalf of the Jews. The combined cities of Buda and Pest were under constant bombardment from the Soviets. Ultimately, Lutz had to hide in the basement of the former British legation building as the buildings around him collapsed into rubble. His leader, Harald Feller, was captured by the Arrow Cross and was just moments away from being executed when a distraction allowed him to escape. Feller was captured by the Soviets in Pest and spent a year in a Soviet prison before diplomats in Bern arranged for his release. Even then, they challenged his support of the Jews in the last days of the war. This caused him so much frustration at the thought that bureaucrats living safely in neutral Switzerland had the temerity to challenge his actions in war-torn Budapest that he resigned from the diplomatic service. Raoul Wallenberg, the courageous Swedish consul, was also captured by the Soviets, and he died in the infamous Lubyanka Prison on Red Square in Moscow, his death never fully explained by his captors.

As previously noted, the guns of war fell silent on January 15, 1945, and Soviet troops moved into the Jewish ghettos, where Lutz's and Wallenberg's extraterritorial safe houses kept the Jews safe. These battle-hardened troops were shocked as emaciated and frightened people emerged from the buildings in numbers that seemed too great to ever fit in the building—starving but grateful that their lives had been spared.

It is estimated that there were 760,000 Jews living in Hungary at the outbreak of World War II. 450,000 were deported to Auschwitz and murdered by the Germans. 100,000 were killed by the Hungarian Arrow Cross and Nyilas. Just 210,000 survived. Swiss consul Carl Lutz is personally credited with saving 62,000 Jews in Hungary in addition to the 10,000 Jewish children he successfully transferred to Palestine for a total of 72,000 saved.

AFTER THE WAR

Immediately after the surrender of Buda, Carl Lutz was forced to leave before he even had a chance to cross the river to Pest to see the people whom he had protected. He was fortunate to find a train to Istanbul, then a steamship to Portugal, from where he ultimately returned to Bern. An official inquiry was called by the Foreign Ministry to see why their vice-consul in Budapest had exceeded his authority in saving the Jews. Fortunately, the judge who oversaw the proceedings recognized his courage and compassion, and Lutz was fully exonerated. The judge even went so far as to chide Lutz's superiors for bringing an action against such a heroic person.

His marriage to Gertrude had ended in divorce. He married one of the women he protected in the American legation building during the war, becoming the stepfather to her daughter. Here is what she had to say about him after his death on February 12, 1975:

"The laws of life are stronger than man-made laws. My father was grown up in a Methodist family in the eastern part of Switzerland and he was the second youngest of ten children. His mother, who was a very strong woman with ethics and social engagement, was the main person and example during his whole life. Later in Budapest, as an engaged Christian he could not tolerate the Jews being pursued and killed, he could not tolerate injustice. He was a deeply religious man and felt he had to protect and help these people. He was not born a hero; he was rather shy and introverted. He launched his mission to save the Jews in Budapest out of his religious and moral convictions. He risked his life and career; he ruined his health working and stressing about the fate of the *Schutzbriefe*-holders day and night. My father always considered his time in Budapest and the rescue of innocent Jews as the most important part of his life."[11]

CHAPTER 6

THE GHOST ARMY

INTRODUCTION

Deception has played an important part in military tactics since man first fought. The American Army, like all other armies, has used it to a more or less degree since the Revolution. General Washington took elaborate pains to mislead the British before his brilliant surprise thrust at Trenton and Princeton in 1777. But it was not until 167 years later that the U.S. Army organized a unit especially trained and equipped for deception.—Captain Fred Fox[1]

Thus begins one of the more interesting stories to emerge out of World War II in the European Theater of Operations; the official history of the highly classified "Ghost Army," which saved an estimated 30,000 American lives through artifice and deception. Organized into five distinct units, the Ghost Army confused the Germans with false radio messages, camouflage, dummy tanks and artillery, "sonic deception" units, and fictional "notional battalions" that deceived German spies. The goal of the 1,100 members of the

Ghost Army was to make the Germans believe that up to two divisions (30,000 US Army troops) were poised to attack in places where there were no troops while drawing German defenders away from places where real American combat units were massing to strike. By reducing the strength of the German resistance, American lives were saved, battle plans were realized faster, and German morale was disrupted and confused. So effective were the 23rd Headquarters Special Troops that both American and British units were also deceived, never realizing that the eccentric characters of the 23rd were placing themselves at mortal risk to help save their units from danger. The Ghost Army was fictional, but the danger was real, since the Germans often fired artillery at the ghost positions and even threatened to attack. Eleven hundred men were no match for the full-strength German divisions that they were plotting to deceive.

At the end of the war in Europe, the 23rd received a special commendation, but were not allowed to talk about their role in the war with anyone—even their own spouses and families—until their official history was declassified in 1966.

As you will see, the 23rd was an unusual complement of men who brought unique talents to bear not often associated with war. Unlike most combat units, the goal of the Ghost Army was to save lives—American and British lives—rather than to kill. After all, they could hardly kill or injure the Nazis with their rubber tanks and phony artillery.

ARTIFICE IN WAR—A FEW EXAMPLES FROM HISTORY

> Although to use deception in any action is detestable, nevertheless in waging war it is praiseworthy and brings fame: he who conquers the enemy by deception is praised as much as he who conquers them by force.—Niccolo Machiavelli[2]

One of the oldest references to artifice (clever or cunning tricks used to deceive) is the legend of the wooden horse built by the Greeks of Sparta in 1200 B.C. to deceive the residents of Troy on the coast of modern-day Turkey. After the Greek king Menelaus discovered that his wife Helen had been kidnapped by Paris of Troy, he waged a ten-year battle against Troy to get her back. But the walls of the city of Troy proved impregnable, and after a decade of fighting the Greeks had failed. That is when the legend says that the Greek general Odysseus came up with a plan of deception. His skilled carpenters constructed a large wooden horse, the symbol of Troy, and inscribed it as a parting gift to the goddess Athena. Feigning defeat, the Greeks left the horse at the gates of Troy and withdrew to their boats on the Aegean Sea, pretending to set sail for home. But one lonely Greek soldier, Sinon, was left behind. When captured by the Trojans, he told them that the horse was built to gain the goddess Athena's favor for a safe return to Greece. To add credibility to the story, he claimed that the tribute was intentionally built too large for the Trojans to bring the horse into the city since it was not meant for them. Feeling euphoric at finally defeating their enemy, the Trojans decided to do just that as a final insult to the Greeks. With great difficulty they dragged the large wooden icon into their city just as dusk fell. What they did not know was that concealed inside the horse were thirty Greek soldiers who, after the Trojans fell asleep, slipped out of the horse and opened the gates to the city for the returning Greek army that had never really retreated. The Greek warriors entered the city and wreaked havoc in a wholesale massacre that ended the war in a victory for Greece. Whether myth or history, the legend of the Trojan Horse shows that the value of deception as a tool of war was well understood by military writers even in ancient times.

In the fifth century B.C., famed Chinese military strategist Sun Tzu included one full chapter on deception in his masterwork *The Art of War*, considered by many as the definitive work on East Asian warfare that continues to influence military policy around the world even today. In a quote that has survived for 2,500 years, he wrote:

"All warfare is based on deception. Hence, when we are able to attack, we must seem unable; when using our forces, we must appear inactive; when we are near, we must make the enemy believe we are far away; when far away, we must make him believe we are near."[3]

A more recent example of deception leading to lives saved comes from the United States War of Independence. In fact, American history might well have remained British history were it not for George Washington's successful use of deception when his army of 10,000 soldiers was surrounded on three sides of the Brooklyn Heights on western Long Island by 20,000 British soldiers led by General William Howe. The British had relentlessly driven Washington back toward the East River, believing that entrapping the Americans with their backs to the water would bring an early end to the Revolutionary War.

Howe's officers urged him to press forward against the Americans, but Howe felt it would be better to lay siege to the heights, slowly starving the Americans into submission with a smaller loss of British lives. After all, he had all the resources of Long Island at his disposal, and the Americans were trapped in a small area with little food and ammunition. A campaign of attrition was just what was called for.

But Howe underestimated the American's cunning. When their plight was fully realized, one of Washington's officers, Thomas Cummings, in command of two Pennsylvania regiments, urged Washington to retreat across the East River on barges while Cummings and his troops conducted rear-guard actions to deceive the British. So it was that on the nights of August 29 and 30, 1776, Washington successfully evacuated his entire army across the surging waters of the East River without Howe having any idea that an escape was in progress. To accomplish this, he had small groups of men make their way back to the river so that most of the troops remained in view of Howe's army. Washington ordered the men to maintain strict silence while moving toward the landing. To accomplish this the soldiers muffled the wheels of their artillery by wrapping them in rags. Once at the river, rags were also used to muffle the sound of the oars in the water as equipment and troops were moved to Manhattan. After dusk fell on the second night, the remainder of the army started a strategic retreat under the cover of darkness. Meanwhile, Thomas Cummings and his Pennsylvanians started numerous campfires, and moved about noisily from abandoned campsite to abandoned campsite to preserve the illusion that the soldiers were still there, cooking their dinners and preparing to retire for the night. When the last of the regulars were across the river, Washington sent word for Cummings and his men to make their escape, which they did in the early hours of August 30, 1776. Washington's army had been saved to fight another day.

Just a few months later, on Christmas Day 1776, Washington used similar tactics in an offensive move when he successfully convinced a large contingent of Hessian mercenaries stationed in Trenton, New Jersey, that Washington's army was too demoralized to mount an attack in the dead of winter. By the careful use of double agents spreading false information and displays of troops skulking sullenly in their camps across the Delaware River, Washington successfully moved the majority of his troops across the icy river in advance of a ten-day assault on Trenton and the surrounding area that completely changed the trajectory of the war.

BRITISH DECEPTION IN WORLD WAR II

By World War II, the British were using deception with great effect. For example, through the use of double agents (German agents sent to spy in Britain, but—after discovery and arrest—secretly "turned" to work for the British), they were able to feed false information to the German spy services. The British also inserted their own spies into German-occupied territories to work with local resistance fighters to send coded information about German troop formations and movements.

Ultra (for "ultra-secret") was the code-name given to a massive British effort to continually intercept and decode German military messages sent by radio to their Enigma code machines in all military theaters. Through skill and deceit, the British broke the code and used the intelligence to anticipate German moves, and occasionally to misdirect German efforts. For example, many thousands of German bombs fell harmlessly in empty fields near British cities because of misdirection.

With respect to creating "ghost armies," the British achieved great success in their military campaigns in North Africa. Multiple disciplines created the illusion of a large army where none existed. For example, the goal of "Operation Bertram" prior to the second Battle of El Alamein in Egypt was to create the impression that British General Montgomery's troops would attack the Germans from the south rather than from their true location north of General Rommel and his troops. This meant that the planners of Bertram had to create two deceptions in the middle of an arid desert, well within sight of German reconnaissance planes: first, to conceal the real army that was massing for the attack; second, to create the false impression of an army group that did not exist to the south of Rommel. They did this using all the methods at their disposal, from dummy tanks to disinformation radio communications. Operation Bertram deceived the Germans into thinking that the British attack would come from the south two days later than the actual attack from the north, an unqualified success.

In another daring deception in April 1943 some Spanish authorities discovered a partially decomposed body floating off the coast of Southern Spain in the Sea of Cadiz, the apparent victim of a plane crash. When they retrieved the corpse, they found papers identifying him as Major William Martin of the Royal Marines. Chained to his wrist was an attaché case. Because Spain was officially a neutral country, proper protocol required them to turn the body over to British authorities without opening the case. As soon as the British learned of the body, they started making frantic diplomatic appeals for its return, but the Spanish hesitated. There were many in the Spanish military who supported the Nazis, and one of them allowed Nazi agents to secretly open the case to examine its contents. Included among the many official documents was a letter to a senior British officer in Tunisia indicating that the British were planning to redeploy their troops in North Africa across the Mediterranean to attack Greece and Sardinia in the east. This intelligence was immediately sent to Berlin, allowing Hitler to move troops from France to Greece in anticipation of the invasion. After all, false radio intercepts had already suggested that the main Allied assault would happen in Greece, so Hitler was predisposed to believe it.

Instead, the British and Americans attacked the island of Sicily on July 10, 1943, rather than Greece. The Germans were woefully unprepared in large part because of the deception employed in placing "Major Martin's" body where it would be discovered by the Spanish authorities.

And who was "Major Martin"? A Welch derelict named Glyndwr Michael who had committed suicide in London. Finding no living relatives, authorities decided to dress his body in a major's uniform, pack it in dry ice, and transport it by submarine to Spain, where it was released into the water where sardine fishermen were sure to discover it. To further the illusion, the British staged an elaborate burial at sea for Major Martin after retrieving the body from Spanish authorities, well within eyesight of German spies who reported the military funeral. And, since London newspapers were monitored by German spies in England, an official death notice of Major William Martin was published soon thereafter. *Ultra* intercepts confirmed that the Germans had swallowed the deception "rod, line, and sinker."[4] This was considered one of the most successful deceptions in the history of war.

These are just a few examples of the many instances in which the British used deception to confuse the enemy. Almost all were successful. But these were really just a prelude to the biggest deception of all that was already being planned and implemented on the southeast coast of England in an operation that involved both the British and Americans.

THE AMERICANS AND BRITISH JOIN FORCES IN OPERATION FORTITUDE

"Camouflage can become a stealth weapon—often showing the enemy what he expects to see, convincing him what he has heard from spies is true, and that what he has seen in photographs is also true."[5]

Hitler's early success in subduing the European mainland meant that an ultimate victory against the Nazis would require the Allies to invade the continent. The obvious place to launch such an invasion was from Dover in southeast England, directly across the English Channel from Pas-de-Calais, France, where the distance across the water was shortest, and the distance from beachhead to Berlin the most direct, which is why Adolf Hitler insisted that the bulk of his European forces be deployed in that area. With enough firepower aimed at an invading armada, there was a good chance the Germans could drive the allies back into the sea.

To avoid this highly risky outcome, the Allies decided to invade the continent from the beaches of Normandy, France, far to the west of Calais, where German resistance was expected to be less fierce. If these plans were discovered, the Germans could respond immediately by redeploying their troops to Normandy. So it was vital that it look like the invasion would launch from Dover and Folkestone across from Calais. But how could they conceal the buildup of more than a million troops in southwest England preparing for the assault on Normandy?

The plan that evolved included two elements. The first was the creation of a fictional United States First Army Group under the command of American General George S. Patton (whom the Germans greatly admired) that would launch the main invasion from southeast England as expected. The second element was to give the illusion of creating a much smaller "diversionary" invasion of Normandy that was intended to draw German forces away from the main assault. In reality, there was no First Army, and the supposedly small buildup of forces in the southwest was really the main invasion force.

To create the illusion of a First Army, phony airfields were created in the southeast with dummy aircraft moved in and out of hangars on a regular basis. Huge dummy landing crafts of various sizes were also created and floated off the coast. Large marshalling yards were built and stocked with dummy tanks, artillery, trucks and even hospital vehicles. The Americans were shocked at how artificial the British dummies looked, wondering if they could really deceive German intelligence with such clumsy facsimiles. But the British had learned early on that while German reconnaissance aircraft had superb optics in their cameras, they shot all their photos in two dimensions. The British always took stereoscopic photos that they could view in 3-D to give a much better appraisal of what was authentic and what was phony.

Also supporting the deployment of the inflatables and wood-and-canvas dummies were real flights by the Royal Air Force in the areas near Dover. They would aggressively chase off German reconnaissance planes whenever they approached, suggesting that there was much the British wished to hide from their prying eyes.

Another important weapon in the Allies toolkit was the use of double agents that they had turned earlier in the war. To preserve the illusion that they were working for the Germans, the British often let them report authentic details. Then, when needed, these agents could send false reports. Also important to the deception was sending important military figures, including General Patton, to where the "First Army" was being staged, making sure that they were visible in a believable way to those who fed the German intelligence apparatus.

Likely the most influential of all deception activities was the judicious use of radio transmissions by the Allies. They sent a vast number of communications from the southeast, while suppressing all but essential communications in the southwest.

The effect of all this was that when Adolf Hitler was shown photos and intelligence signaling a large build-up of forces in the southwest across from Normandy, he was not surprised, thinking it was the diversionary move. He became so convinced of an invasion at Pas-de-Calais that he stubbornly refused to allow any of his Panzer tank units to be moved without his express authority. This proved disastrous to the Germans when the assault on Europe was launched on D-Day, June 6, 1944, against the five Normandy beaches.

To say that Operation Fortitude was a success is an understatement. For nearly three months after the D-Day landings, Hitler continued to refuse urgent requests from his generals to move the Panzer units to Normandy. This delay gave the Americans and British enough time and room to establish a beachhead and to start reinforcing it. More than one million Allied troops made the crossing to France before the Germans finally accepted that there was no invasion coming at Calais. Only then did Hitler allow the Panzers and supporting troops to move west, but it was too late. The Americans and British were firmly on the mainland and Germany would be put on the defensive from that point forward. But now a new type of deception was needed.

The stationary British wood-and-canvas decoys were too

cumbersome and crude to work effectively in the dynamic new environment of active warfare on the continent. If deception were to be used in the liberation of Europe it would need to be agile and mobile, ready to move at a moment's notice, a ghost army appearing and then disappearing in just a matter of days. It would need to be customized to land-based battles fought near rivers and in forests where the enemy was sometimes within a few hundred yards of where the deception was taking place. It called for entirely new strategies, and it was to these challenges that American ingenuity would respond in spectacular fashion. It was time for the 23rd to play its role in achieving victory in Europe.

COMMISSIONING THE 23RD

"The Ghost Army's role was as a top-secret mobile group assigned wherever a deception was needed, a sleight-of-hand required, or an army of 30,000 soldiers had to be impersonated. The vanished combat unit was replaced by a handful of artists, actors, carpenters, electricians, sound trucks, rubber and pasteboard tanks, inflatable artillery, a cardboard air force and bogus radio communications. In most cases, this mythical band's job was to draw fire and attention from the Germans while the actual fighting force appeared—as if by magic— on that enemy's unprotected flank. Other operations required them to sound like rolling thunder at the enemy's front, a boiling mass of guns and tanks, surging at the leash behind the black of night, or hidden by a billowing cloud of fog."[6]

The idea for military units specifically dedicated to deception was introduced to the United States command structure as early as 1941 by Hollywood superstar Douglas Fairbanks, Jr. He was sent as a member of the US Navy Reserve to England at the request of Lord Louis Mountbatten to temporarily join Mountbatten's command. While in England, Fairbanks learned of attempts in the British Navy to use sonic deception by recording the sounds of a seaborne invasion. They hoped to use mobile loudspeakers to play those sounds from fast motor torpedo boats off an enemy coast in an area where the invasion was *not* to take place in order to draw attention from where a commando raid *was* taking place. Fairbanks, who had played a swashbuckler in many Hollywood movies, participated in practice drills off Scotland and was enthralled by the idea.

On Fairbanks's return to the United States, he recommended the strategy to Washington, DC. In time, this led to a top-secret letter from Admiral Ernest King, chief of naval operations, for the recruitment of 180 officers and 300 enlisted men to create the "Beach Jumper" program, which ultimately created diversionary landings during the Allied invasion of Sicily and successfully drew German fire away from the actual landings. The Beach Jumpers continued to provide support for other naval actions through the end of the war. Fairbanks received numerous military awards from Allied nations for his role in helping create and participate in this unit, including the US Navy's Legion of Merit with a Bronze V for Valor.

While not part of the Ghost Army, the Beach Jumpers were a source of inspiration for the creation of the 23rd Headquarters Special Troops on December 24, 1943, by order of General Jake Devers, commander of the European Theater of Operations. The Ghost Army was activated on January 20, 1944, at Camp Forrest, Tennessee, under the command of Colonel Harry L. Reeder. While the command was new, it quickly absorbed four operational units that were already working on deception activities.

The **603rd Engineer Camouflage Battalion** was mainly comprised of artists and architects, many from New York and Philadelphia. Their task was to use their artistic skills to create dummy equipment, including remarkably lifelike inflatable tanks and artillery that could be quickly placed and removed in the field. Prior to leaving for England, artists in the group worked with American rubber manufacturers to perfect the inflatables so they could be carried in canvas bags but would look completely authentic when inflated. These were not large balloons—they used multiple elements to provide rigidity needed to maintain their shape in all types of weather and remain inflated even if one section was torn by enemy shrapnel. The American inflatables were far superior to what the British had created to that point in time.

Members of the 603rd also became highly skilled at changing the command insignia on troop transports, uniform patches, and other unit identification to disguise when a unit was moving to a new, secret location. This also required them to pass themselves off as generals, colonels, and even military police by circulating in towns along the route where they bantered in front of the locals to complete the deception. The average IQ of this group was in the borderline genius range; many went on to distinguished careers after the war as artists and designers, including fashion designer Bill Blass and painter-sculptor Ellsworth Kelly. The battalion was comprised of twenty-eight officers, two warrant officers, and 349 enlisted men.

The **244th Signal Operations Company** was responsible for creating vast amounts of radio counterintelligence. More than 100 of the top radio operators in all theaters of the war were reassigned to this group so that they could learn to imitate the communications style of every operational battalion in Europe. For example, each Morse code operator has a unique touch—almost like a fingerprint. To imitate an operator, the members of the 244th would listen in on their pattern for several days and then begin mixing their messages with the operator. When the operational unit withdrew, the Germans were completely unaware that the new operators had been replaced with others sending phony messages. The 244th used Morse code, radio, teletype, and wire messages in their deception. The strength of this unit was eleven officers and 349 enlisted men.

The **406th Engineer Combat Company** was comprised of active Army combat engineers whose task was to support the deception units of the 23rd. They operated the transport trucks and bulldozers, built the huts and phony airfields, and set up new headquarters whenever the 23rd received a new assignment. In time, however, they became active in the deception plans in addition to their regular duties by supporting the camouflage units. For example, it's one thing to inflate a highly realistic neoprene Sherman tank in a field, but to make it look real from the air required tracks from the road to the place where the dummy was stationed. The 406th Engineers would carefully drive bulldozers to the spot, then reverse course precisely so that from the air it looked like the inflatable tank had driven there. The 406th also supported the sonic unit by adding their own heavy equipment sounds. This unit had five officers and 163 enlisted men.

The **3132nd Signal Service Company** was responsible for sonic deception. It was organized separately from other units at the Army Experimental Station in Pine Camp, New York. According to the official history of the unit, their role was "more theatrical than military." They spent a great deal of time in the United States building a library of recordings of armored and artillery units setting up or breaking camp in a new location.

While earlier attempts at sonic deception had used vinyl records, which was state-of-the art at the time, the 3132nd used metal wire recorders to provide stability in the field while their sound trucks were in motion. To make their recordings completely authentic, they recorded tanks, trucks, and artillery moving in all weather conditions in a variety of terrains.

Their recordings included the sound of Army sergeants yelling at their subordinates, just as they would in a real encampment. The technicians of the 3132nd were early innovators in using stereo recordings so that the sound of a tank passing a location would create the correct sound profile.

Their library was an impressive collection of special effects, which would be supplemented with real vehicles and flash grenades to simulate the sounds and sight of tanks and artillery firing. The sound façade deceived the Germans—as well as Allied troops—into thinking a full battalion of 66,000-pound Sherman tanks or a 15,000-man division was moving into or out of an area, when in reality it was just a handful of sound trucks with loudspeaker arrays that could blast their sound effects for up to fifteen miles. This unit had eight officers and 137 enlisted men.

The 23rd Headquarters Company were the senior officers and support staff of the 23rd Special Operations Troops. In total, 1,100 men were assigned to the 23rd with the task of imitating up to 30,000 regular combat troops, depending on what the situation required. It was an awesome and dangerous responsibility—and one that the creative minds of this unique army relished.

THE GHOST ARMY GOES INTO BATTLE

After extensive training in the United States and deploying to England prior to the D-Day assault on Normandy, the first units of the 23rd embarked for France within days of the landings at Omaha and Utah Beach. But because they were not mission-critical to the initial assault, it took two months and nine ships to get all 1,100 men into France.

The best way to appreciate the role the Ghost Army played in the liberation of Europe is through the missions they completed.

Operation Brest took place between August 20–27, 1944. After the Normandy landings in the northwest corner of France, the Germans still controlled the western French port of Brest, giving the Nazis access to the Atlantic Ocean. From there, German U-boats disrupted British supply lines to the Mediterranean and harassed troop convoys from America. The Americans committed to attack the port by land from the east. In Operation Brest the 23rd used their camouflage and radio skills to make it seem that the Allied forces were stronger by more than a full division (15,000 soldiers). Operation Brest was the first time the 23rd used their five sonic half-track vehicles within 500 yards of the enemy, projecting tank noise while fifty dummy tanks mixed with real tanks, artillery, tents, and laundry were positioned nearby for spies to see. So authentic were their efforts that US forces a mile away were convinced that a full American tank division had assembled in the area.

Another part of the operation placed dummy flash batteries 800 yards in front of the US 37th Field Artillery Battalion intending to draw enemy fire to the phony artillery instead of the 37th's howitzers. For the three nights of August 23 through August 25 the dummy units received heavy enemy fire—and the real battalion received none. At the end of this campaign, Colonel Cyrus H. Searcy, chief of staff for VIII Corps, wrote that "the work of these deception units is complete, thorough and correct to the smallest detail. It is believed that units of this type are of considerable value to the Army."[7]

With the fall of Brest, the Germans were driven back east toward Germany. American troops celebrated when Paris was liberated on August 25, 1944. This allowed the 23rd to transfer to Versailles, near Paris, to assist where the units of the Twelfth Army Group were converging; the First Army on the north of Paris, the Third Army commanded by General George S. Patton from the south, and the Seventh Army coming up from the invasion of the French Riviera on the Mediterranean Sea. While stationed in Versailles, the men of the 23rd put on talent shows in a makeshift "Blarney Theater" where they imitated the Abbott and Costello movie *Ghostbreakers*, but with a slightly different plot each of four nights. They also enjoyed the jubilant atmosphere of liberated Paris when they could wrangle a leave of absence.

But the war moved quickly, and the 23rd was uprooted from their posh surroundings in Versailles and moved to the Luxembourg city of Metz, where the First and Third Armies had both ground to a halt because of stiffening German resistance.

The 23rd engaged in **Operation Bettembourg**, September 15–22, when the First Army stalled at the Siegfried Line north of Luxembourg and the Third Army halted at the Moselle River. A seventy-mile gap was opened between them that could easily be exploited by the Germans. The 23rd was sent into this gap to pretend to be the 6th Armored Division. Their goal was to draw the enemy away from Metz as well as to make it appear that the 43rd Cavalry was at greater strength. While the diversion was supposed to last just sixty hours, the 23rd was held in the gap, extremely vulnerable to enemy fire, for a full seven days. It was in Operation Bettembourg that every unit of the 23rd was called on to display their talents. Four types of deception were used: radio, dummies, sonic, and special effects. The radio operators made it appear that ten radios were active in the area when only three were real. Twenty-three decoys were placed to create the deception of armor in the gap. The sonic company played the sound of tanks rumbling about in a variety of operations for four of the six nights of the deployment. Meanwhile, the actors of the group, dressed in the uniforms of the 6th Armored with authentic patches, vehicles bumper markings, military police uniforms, and a phony major general who made himself visible to the locals in Metz, some of whom were collaborating with the Nazis.

Men in the 23rd were sent in 6th Armored uniforms into nearby towns to attend church, take showers, visit taverns and restaurants, and just generally act the part of an invading army. They had been given a quick tutorial in the history of the division so that they could give authentic answers if asked questions by either locals or active Allied units in the area. The success of Operation Bettembourg was confirmed when it was learned that the Germans had given the real 6th Armored the nickname "Phantom Division."

As the front moved north from Luxembourg, the 23rd was called on to cover for the 5th Armored Division as it moved sixty miles north in **Operation Wiltz 4**. The goal was to make the Germans believe the 5th was moving, but not as far north as it intended to go. This would force the Germans to keep defensive troops in the wrong place, allowing the 5th to complete a surprise flanking maneuver against the enemy when they were fully repositioned.

The 23rd set up a "notional" division thirty-five miles south of the actual position of the 5th Armored, using primarily fake radio traffic and actors to deceive the Germans. Seventeen radios were deployed over an area of 1,000 square miles. To make the deception believable, two days before the operation began, radio operators from the 23rd began operating alongside the 5th Armored's radio operators, learning their unique Morse code signatures. Then the 5th Armored moved north under radio silence, and the phony traffic of the 23rd fooled the enemy. Germans captured after the operation confirmed that their commanders had believed the deception.

In **Operation Elsenborn**, November 3–12, 1944, the 23rd operated twenty-two transmitters using 100 operators around the clock to cover a multitude of moves by various army groups. The main move they covered was the withdrawal of the 4th Infantry Division by simulating radio traffic from a full notional division in what had been the 4th Infantry's Elsenborn barracks. The camouflage and special effects units assisted by posting misleading road signs and mismarked jeeps and transports. They were so convincing that nearby US units were fully convinced the 4th Infantry was still at Elsenborn. Some late-arriving officers from the 4th were surprised to see unfamiliar faces in their barracks. "When the 4th finally jumped off into the terrible woods of Hurtgen, it is said that the enemy was surprised by their presence,"[8] as evidenced by a German map overlay that showed them still at Elsenborn.

At mostly the same time, **Operation Dallas**, November 2–10, 1944, was a chance for the camouflage battalion to show their stuff in Jarny, France. For eight days they maintained inflated dummy armor and artillery next to real artillery batteries to make the batteries seem larger than they were. The XX Corps left 500 men and twelve guns, supplemented by 195 men from the 23rd with thirty-six dummy artillery pieces and multiple art flashes to replace 2,230 men and forty-eight guns that had been moved out of the area. The mock flashes were coordinated with authentic fire orders from the remaining artillery to make it appear as if full battalion concentrations were firing. To complete the illusion, air patrols continued to fly above the line, sending adjustments to the firing patterns. While it was not ascertained if the Germans were deceived by Operation Dallas, it was documented that plenty of Americans in nearby emplacements were fooled.

On December 6, 1944, the Germans employed their own deception to launch a fierce counterattack against Allied positions in what became known as the Battle of the Bulge. Called the "greatest American battle of the war" by Winston Churchill, the rapid advance of Allied troops since the D-Day landing six months earlier ground to a halt. The Allies fought Germany on multiple fronts in the midst of the coldest winter recorded in European history. With a constantly changing battlefront, it was natural that the Ghost Army would be called on to pretend to fill gaps in the line while real fighting units were repositioned in an ever-changing order of battle. **Operation Metz 2** took place January 6–19, 1945. One of the most important missions the 23rd undertook was to make it appear by radio alone that the 90th Infantry was still holding in their position near Thionville while they moved to assist the liberation of American forces at Bastogne, Belgium.

The Americans in Bastogne had been encircled by the Germans but were holding out in desperate circumstances under intense enemy fire. The 23rd needed to make it appear the 90th was still in place until they were replaced by the 94th Infantry that was moving in from Lorient. Appropriate phony radio traffic covered the withdrawal, while the special effects group worked hard to imitate the 90th in the area, using bumper identification on their vehicles, shoulder patches, and road signs to indicate that 90th was still active. Meanwhile, the real 90th Infantry performed magnificently in the rescue of the soldiers in Bastogne.

Operation Flaxweiler, January 17–18, 1945, allowed the sound trucks to use a new set of recordings of bridge building across a river. The XII Corp planned to cross the Moselle River near Diekirch, Luxembourg, so the sound engineers of the 23rd's 3132nd Signal Service Company created a false crossing twenty miles to the south of the real operation. The 2nd Cavalry displayed bridge building materials in the diversionary area and the 23rd's sound trucks augmented the deception with the noise of bridge construction. Other sound units raced up and down the Allied side of the river blasting out the sound of tanks arriving. This led to an increase in enemy artillery fire on this false position, thus drawing resistance away from the actual crossing.

The success of the 23rd's deceptions improved drastically with increased coordination with operating units. General George Patton was more likely than most to request assistance from the 23rd for troop movements in eastern France and made sure that the 23rd had the support they needed to create effective diversions. By the early months of 1945, as the Allies prepared to invade Germany, successful collaborations were the rule, not the exception. Which is why the 23rd was so well prepared to tackle its most important deception operation of the war—and the one that would turn out to be its last.

Operation Viersen ran March 18–24, 1945. "The objective as stated in the official report was: 'As part of a Ninth US Army deception plan, to deceive the enemy as to the actual Rhine River crossing area, strength of the crossing and time of crossing.' The specific mission was: 'To simulate the 30th and 79th Infantry assembling in

XVI Corps zone, and furnish advice on the Army cover plan as well as technique of deception to Commanding General, XIII Corps.' The beauty of this operation lay in three facts: (1) the contribution of the 23rd was only a part of a giant spectacle involving practically all of the real Ninth Army; (2) the 23rd had reached its highest state of efficiency and all of its deceptive strength was employed; (3) from all evidences, the operation was a success."[9]

The Rhine is one of the great rivers of the world, running south to north from Switzerland to the North Sea near Amsterdam. For most of its 766 miles it forms the border between France and Germany. Not only is it an imposing physical barrier between the two countries, it held enormous psychological value in the Allies' campaign to defeat the Germans. Crossing the Rhine would bring the war onto German soil.

In the early days of the war, German lines were stretched across tens of thousands of miles, troops deployed in North Africa, Greece, France and the Low Countries, Norway, and across the vast Russian frontier. But as the Allies advanced on Germany's borders, the Nazi supply lines were tighter and they could increase the concentration of troops all along the line to resist invasion. In other words, they were growing stronger rather than weaker with each mile recaptured by the Allies.

Preventing the Allies from bridging the Rhine thus became one of Hitler's primary objectives. Troops crossing in boats and combat engineers working in the river were sitting ducks for German aircraft and artillery. If German leadership could ascertain exactly where and when the Allies intended to establish their bridgeheads, they could unleash all the fury of their troops who were now fighting for their homeland. That is why deception was so important for saving American and British lives and successfully crossing the river.

Operation Viersen was named for a small German town near where the phony invasion was supposed to take place, north of the actual crossing planned by the Ninth Army. The operational army moved in strict silence and under cover of darkness, using extensive camouflage to hide their combat engineer staging parks. The XIII notional unit, on the other hand, went out of their way to make noise, display dummy tanks, create obvious staging parks for notional combat engineers, partially camouflage bridge-building equipment, and use sound trucks suggesting that intense activity was taking place. Real artillery was mixed in with the inflatable dummies to fire on German positions on the east bank of the river. Antiaircraft artillery was simulated with sixty-four 40mm and sixteen 90mm rubber guns furnished by the 603rd Engineers of the Ghost Army. Men of the 23rd actively patrolled near the frontlines in the XIII's fictional staging area to add authenticity. The sounds of bridge building equipment were broadcast by the 500-pound speakers on the sound trucks. A spoof radio network created false traffic reports suggesting a large increase in vehicle movement in the area.

For this important operation, the 23rd pulled out all the stops, utilizing every means of deception available. Each notional division had nearly 400 extra rubber vehicles. The 23rd created phony airfields with phony airplanes, all of which looked authentic when photographed from the air. To the Germans listening in on their radios and hearing vehicle traffic across the river, it seemed assured that the Rhine crossing was scheduled to take place on April 1, 1945, at Viersen.

Which is why the Ninth Army achieved complete surprise when it launched the real crossing at 2:00 A.M. on March 24, 1945, between Rhineberg and Rees—not at Viersen as the Germans had been led to believe. The crossing was preceded by 7,500 air sorties against the Germans supported by heavy artillery fire from concealed positions. The authentic staging parks that had been concealed by camouflage came alive with activity as the bridge builders began their work.[10]

Though it was classified top secret until 1966, the commanding officer of the Twelfth Army Group wrote a letter of commendation to the 23rd as follows:

> HEADQUARTERS
> NINTH UNITED STATES ARMY
> 29 March 1945
> SUBJECT: Commendation
> TO: Commanding Officer, 23rd Headquarters Special Troops, Twelfth Army Group.
> THROUGH: Commanding General, Twelfth Army Group
>
> 23rd Headquarters Special Troops, Twelfth Army Group, was attached to NINTH US Army on 15 March 1945 to participate in the operation to cross the Rhine River.
>
> The unit was engaged in a special project, which was an important part of the operation. The careful planning, minute attention to detail, and diligent execution of the tasks to be accomplished by the personnel of the organization reflect great credit on this unit.
>
> I desire to commend the officers and men of the 23rd Headquarters Special Troops, Twelfth Army Group, for their fine work and to express my appreciation for a job well done.
>
> / s / t / W.H. SIMPSON
> Lt. General, US Army
> Commanding[11]

The 30th G-2 (military intelligence) said of Operation Viersen that the US attack came as a complete surprise to the enemy with a consequent saving of American lives. German maps captured after the action showed that the Germans had expected the assault exactly where the 23rd had set up their ghost army, and that they had lost track of the actual bridging force entirely.

WINDING UP THE 23RD

Once American forces were inside Germany, the need for deception activities of the 23rd ended. The psychological blow to German forces was severe, and the next two months saw a chaotic retreat and mass surrender by German troops in the face of determined Allied advances. When victory in Europe was declared on May 8, 1945, the Ghost Army was taking on new roles as military police guarding refugee camps filled with displaced persons (refugees) from twenty-six nations. Some members of the 23rd acted as camp managers while others assisted in directing food and medical care to the suffering refugees.

As these activities were taken over by other Army units or by local civilian leaders, the 23rd began preparing for redeployment to the Pacific Theater to continue the fight against the Japanese. The main units of the Ghost Army transferred by troop transport to Rouen, France, prior to boarding a troopship for the United States. Here is what the official historian of the 23rd wrote about their transfer home:

"The rain, purges, inspections, and training schedules could have been quite agonizing if the glorious sunlight of HOME! had not peeked through every dark cloud. It took about three days for the happy 23rd convoys to motor from Idar-Obserstein to the staging area near Rouen. . . . France never looked so beautiful. The wheat was ripe and mixed with poppies and bluebells. To men dizzy with thoughts of home, every field could have been a rippling flag—or the neon lights of Broadway, a colorful county fair, a Mardi-Gras, or a whirling rodeo in Flagstaff, Arizona. . . .

"The good boat left from Le Havre. It was called the *General O.H. Ernst* and sailed for America alone and with lights on 23 June 1945. The voyage was smooth, the quarters clean, the prospects glorious. It was a Navy transport and the Army passengers were impressed by the efficiency and good spirit. Sgt. Alfred Berry took over the library again; Corporal Teddy Katz led his famous orchestra and Sergeant Seymour Kent produced a number of extravaganzas built around two Red Cross girls. Everyone else bathed in the sun."[12]

The ship arrived in Newport News, Virginia, on July 2, 1945. Most of the men departed for a thirty-day leave to return home and see their family and friends prior to departing to the South Pacific to take up action against the Japanese. But with the dropping of the atomic bombs at Nagasaki and Hiroshima, the Japanese surrendered on August 14, 1945, and World War II came to an end. The unit was to be fully deactivated by September 15, 1945. The 23rd Headquarters Special Troops came to an end on September 10th when Captain Frederick E. Fox completed his official history of the 23rd:

"On 10 September the 23rd Adjutant told your 87-pointed historian that the only thing that kept him from being released was the completion of this story. So now it's done and tomorrow I will be a free man again. The End. Frederick E. Fox 01–634769 Captain AUS Sig O. retired."[13]

It's not often that an active-duty soldier gets to declare himself "retired." The remarkable story of the 23rd, including those who were killed and those who were wounded, could not be shared with anyone including spouses and family until Fred Fox's history was declassified twenty-one years later. Only then did the world learn the full truth of thirty-ton Sherman tanks that could be hoisted into the air by four men, of sound trucks with massive speaker arrays that could duplicate the sound of a mechanized army on the move, or of artists and actors who impersonated senior officers while intentionally disobeying the injunction "loose lips sink ships" in order to deceive local German sympathizers into thinking that a US Army unit or division was someplace that it was not. The Ghost Army finally came alive for history to remember and appreciate.

CHAPTER 7

THE BATTLE FOR CASTLE ITTER

INTRODUCTION

"Halfway between Berchtesgaden, Germany, and Innsbruck, Austria, ten kilometers south of the town of Wörgl lies the medieval castle of Itter which has been used as a VIP (Very-Important-Persons) prisoner-of-war camp since 1943 and now houses the most valuable French hostages.

"On 5 May 1945 there is a short battle for the castle which is unparalleled in the history of the Second World War, but nevertheless typical—from the Allied viewpoint—of the fighting spirit they always expected from German SS troops in the alpine stronghold.

"Prisoners held there include two former French Premiers, Paul Reynaud and Edouard Daladier; Andrew Francois Poncet, former French ambassador in Berlin; Chief of the French General Staff General Gamelin, as well as General Weygand; Mme Caillou, sister of General de Gaulle with her husband; Jean Borotra, a former Vichy Minister and well-known tennis star, and Michel Clemenceau, son of the famous French statesman.

"*They are all aware of Himmler's order that all hostages are to be shot before Allied troops arrive,* and they await their last hour behind stout castle walls, barbed wire, and dozens of searchlights guarded by sentries and dogs.

"When an American tank arrives on 5 May 1945 . . . shots are fired from the surrounding woods, and the castle is encircled by 300 SS-men who have come to execute Kaltenbrunner's order to shoot the hostages."[1]

The Battle of the Bulge, from December 16, 1944, through January 25, 1945, was Nazi Germany's last major counterattack of the war. After that, the Allied armies made steady progress in forcing German troops to retreat on all fronts, with the ultimate objective of capturing Berlin and ending the war. By April 30, 1945, it was clear that Germany was defeated—so clear, in fact, that Adolf Hitler committed suicide just a few blocks from the smoking ruins of the German Parliament building. This news spread quickly even among German troops, who now knew that the war was lost. Most wanted to stop fighting immediately and to quickly find a way to return to their homes instead of to Allied prisoner-of-war camps.

But not the Waffen-SS troopers who were fanatically loyal to Hitler even after his death. Taken from their families as children, the Waffen-SS were elite military units that had been trained for just one purpose—to serve Hitler and the Nazi cause without regard to their own personal needs, desires, or safety. Now they lusted for revenge and would sooner fight to the death than surrender—while taking as many Allied troops and prisoners with them as possible.

In a cruel twist of fate, the time of greatest danger to those imprisoned in Nazi concentration camps was in the few days leading up to Germany's unconditional surrender on May 8, 1945, because many of the camp commanders wanted to destroy the evidence of their crimes against humanity and to complete Hitler's goal of killing all Jews and other "undesirables" while they could. It was in this overheated atmosphere that SS-Reichsführer Heinrich Himmler ordered that all prisoners in SS prison camps be executed before hostilities ceased. The last battle of the war would be fought in the Tyrol region of Austria and threatened the lives of some of the most influential prisoners ever held in wartime.

CASTLE ITTER

Just seventy miles south of Munich, Germany, sits the small Tyrolean village of Itter, Austria. Located in a beautiful alpine valley, it abuts the Austrian Alps in a narrow gorge that is ideally suited as a defensive battlement. Which is why, in 902 A.D., a Roman fortress was built in Itter. In the intervening centuries, several structures were built on the site that over time became home to royalty as well as various bishops and archbishops of the Catholic Church, even serving as the summer residence of the pope for several decades.

In 1812 the castle fell to Napoleon Bonaparte, who claimed it as a prize of war. The current medieval fairytale-like castle was built in 1878. One of Europe's most acclaimed pianists, Sophie Menter, turned it into a music conservatory and invited such luminaries as Tchaikovsky, Wagner, and Liszt to use her magnificent home as a retreat. She later sold the castle to a wealthy Berliner who updated the castle with electricity, indoor plumbing, and other refinements and turned it into a luxury mountain hotel.[2]

By 1943 the castle had passed through several more owners, the last of whom reluctantly turned the castle over to the Waffen-SS to be converted into an "honors prison" for high-profile French prisoners. These prisoners were held as bargaining chips by Hitler to use in negotiating prisoner exchanges or for gaining other concessions from the Allies as the war developed.

THE PRISONERS

The first French dignitaries/prisoners arrived at Castle Itter in January 1943, with more coming over the course of the next two years. They were treated with great respect by the German guards and had remarkable access to the news of the outside world. Former French Prime Minister Edouard Daladier wrote in his journal of reading the *Times* of London and the Manchester *Guardian*. The prisoners were aware of the major battles of the war, including actions in North Africa, Greece, Russia, the Balkans, and eventually the invasion of France at Normandy. They could also listen to German language broadcasts, including Hitler's final speech to the German people on the radio. And they were often apprised of happenings in both Paris and Vichy France. They even had interactions with the people of the village of Itter:

"April 23, 1944. Spring has made a modest appearance in the Tirol; the light is playing upon the snow-covered mountaintops. What a wonderful morning! Suddenly, at 10 A.M. there was an explosion in the village. From behind my barred window, I watched as a villager in a deserted street prepared to fire another round from the cannon that they use to signal the joyous or painful events that mark village life. More blasts shook the air. I learned that the cannon shots had been occasioned by the news that two of their sons had died on the battlefield. Then the church bell began to toll. I understand that the priest gave a moving talk and that all the women gathered in prayer were in tears. Itter has a population of only 400; 12 of them are now dead. Proportionately, that works out to 2 million deaths for Germany."[3]

The French luminaries who were imprisoned at Castle Itter were, in many cases, bitter political enemies. While Charles de Gaulle's older sister, Marie Cailliau, thought they should all get along with each other to present a united front to the Germans, it just was not to be.

"American Major Kramers whistled through his mustache and called the division's French liaison officer, Lt. Eric Lutten, who studied the list of prisoners and remarked on the *psychic cruelty* of which the Germans were capable. To lock up in one castle a group such as this! A labor leader and a Fascist leader, two prime ministers and the generals who had failed them, a Vichy cabinet member, and the sister of the leader of French resistance.

"But certainly, those French personalities had to be rescued—some of them because they deserved freedom; others because the French state would want an explanation of their conduct. Yes, the cast of Itter contained a hatful!"[4]

Eventually the fourteen VIP prisoners sorted themselves into three groups, each hostile to the others.

First, the Daladier group:

Edouard Daladier had been the French premier in 1933, then minister of National Defense and War in 1936, and premier a second time from April 10, 1938 through March 21, 1940. He, along with British Prime Minister Neville Chamberlain, had signed the infamous Munich non-aggression pact with Adolf Hitler in 1938, only to declare war on Germany a year later. He was replaced as premier in 1940 by his bitter political enemy Paul Reynaud. As the Germans closed in on Paris, Daladier and other ministers sailed to Casablanca to set up a French government-in-exile. But his reception there was chilly, and he was held under house arrest until after July 10, 1940, when the new pro-Nazi government in France accepted the German armistice and installed Marshal Philippe Pétain as premier in unoccupied Vichy.[5] Daladier returned to France, where he was arrested along with Paul Reynaud and others to be prosecuted for failing to protect France from Nazi Germany.

Leon Jouhaux was a prominent labor leader who, after France's defeat, joined the Vichy government to provide legitimacy to the new government with the labor unions. But Jouhaux soon became disillusioned with the Germans, refusing to work with them. He was arrested by the Gestapo for his stubbornness. He was in poor health when incarcerated at age sixty-one.

Augusta Bruchlen was Leon Jouhaux's assistant and romantic partner. She orchestrated her own arrest so she could come to Itter to look after Jouhaux and to continue their relationship.

Marie-Agnes Cailliau was the older sister of General Charles de Gaulle, leader of the Free French forces in North Africa during the war and leader of France's liberation forces after the Normandy landings. Charles became president of the Provisional Government of France from 1944 through 1946 and then president of the French Republic from 1958 through 1968. Marie was arrested with her husband because of her relationship to de Gaulle. The Nazis believed they could exert influence over General de Gaulle because of her captivity.

Alfred Cailliau was Marie Cailliau's husband; a Belgian by birth, he was an engineer. After his marriage to Marie, they moved to Le Havre, where they raised six sons and a daughter. At the outbreak of World War II one of their sons was killed, and the four older sons joined the resistance. Trying to protect their youngest son, they moved south to Lyon to live with their daughter. Here they supported one of their older sons in his clandestine resistance work. When they returned north, they were arrested. At first, they assumed that their subversive activities had been discovered. But they were arrested simply because of Marie's relationship to Charles de Gaulle. Alfred suffered a great deal of torture and deprivation while in prison at Buchenwald before his transfer to Castle Itter.

Marcel Granger had been arrested by the French Milice (the Vichy militia who collaborated with the Germans) for espionage against the Nazis in French Tunisia. He was saved from execution by a sister-in-law, the daughter of French Army General Henri Giraud, who had escaped German captivity and was helping the

Allies. Granger and other Giraud family members were imprisoned in order to blackmail the general into returning to the German side, perhaps as a double agent. Granger had been a witness to many atrocities at the Dachau concentration camp and shared his horror stories with the other French prisoners after arriving in Castle Itter.

Second, the Reynaud Group:

Paul Reynaud, a political enemy of Daladier, succeeded him as premier of France, serving just three months from March 1940 through June 16, 1940. He fled Paris two days after the Germans took the city. Reynaud made the choice to elevate eighty-four-year-old Marshal Philippe Pétain, a World War I military hero, as the premier of Vichy France. When Pétain began collaborating with the Nazis, many of France's prior leaders were furious with Reynaud for his decision. He ran afoul of the Germans, who ordered his arrest and transfer to Itter.

Christine Mabire had been Paul Reynaud's assistant, just twenty-seven years old when he appointed her. She had a romantic affair with him while he was married. When Reynaud's wife was killed in a car accident, Reynaud agitated to have Mabire sent to join him in Itter. She was thirty-five years younger than Reynaud during their imprisonment.

General **Maurice Gamelin** had been chief of the French Army general staff, and failed to defend France when Germany invaded on May 10, 1940. Reynaud replaced Gamelin with Maxime Weygand. When French military resistance collapsed under the Nazi onslaught, both Reynaud and Gamelin blamed Weygand for surrendering too quickly, thus becoming unlikely allies against a common foe.

Michel Clemenceau was the third child of the French Premier Georges Clemenceau who had led France during World War I. Michel was a decorated veteran of World War I and a successful businessman. He opposed Marshal Pétain's Vichy government, but felt that he would be safe from arrest because of his political connections, even though he sent his wife to live in America in November 1940. But he was wrong about his safety and was arrested by the Nazis in May 1943 when they occupied Vichy France. The Nazis viewed Clemenceau's family name as a potential asset in future negotiations with the French. Michel spent many months in French and German prisons before being transferred to Castle Itter in January 1945. He was an optimistic person who got along well with all three groups, though he took his meals with the Reynaud group. Many of the other prisoners appreciated his steadying influence with the prisoners.

Third, the Weygand Group:

General **Maxime Weygand** replaced Maurice Gamelin as chief of the Army general staff in the last weeks of French army resistance against the German army. He was one of the architects of the French Armistice with Germany, and then worked with the Vichy government after France was partitioned into occupied and unoccupied zones. For this, he was bitterly resented by both Daladier and Reynaud as well as his predecessor Gamelin. When he arrived at Castle Itter, Paul Reynaud muttered, "Traitor, collaborator!"[6] Weygand claimed that he had helped craft the treaty to save French lives, and to perhaps live to fight another day. Despite his cooperation with both the Germans and the Vichy government, he eventually fell out of favor with Adolf Hitler after the Allied landings in North Africa. Reynaud was arrested at age seventy-six along with his wife, **Marie Renee Josephine Weygand**.

Jean Borotra was an internationally acclaimed tennis star who had been appointed commissioner for sports by the Vichy government, with the goal of making life as normal as possible for the French, including its young people. He was angered when told that he could not include French Jews in the teams he organized, and outraged when asked to help in the roundup of Jews in Paris. He was summoned to the German embassy in Paris in April 1942, where he adamantly refused to exclude "undesirables" from French sports programs. The Nazis ordered him fired, and he was arrested in November 1942 while attempting to escape France to join the Allies. At Castle Itter he ran every day around the interior courtyard to keep up his physical conditioning. This would prove helpful when he needed to escape the castle to seek American help in May 1945.

Francois de la Rocque was a prominent Fascist and a member of the Vichy government. Many Frenchmen considered him a traitor. What they did not know is that he was secretly a member of the French Resistance, sending crucial information to London and Madrid through the Alibi network. He was descended from a French noble family and would have held the title Viscount of Chateaubriand in the days of the monarchy. His clandestine activities were discovered and he was arrested by the Gestapo, leading to his transfer to Castle Itter in January 1944.

These three groups made up the contingent of fourteen well-fed, well-treated prisoners at Castle Itter as the war drew to an end. Each were given their own apartment with electricity, running water, and toilet. They shared group meals prepared by a chef and could read anything they liked in the castle's extensive library. While not allowed to leave the castle, they could exercise in the interior courtyard as desired. Yet they all lived under the knowledge that they could be traded like pawns in a chess game anytime the Nazis liked—even killed if it served the Nazis' purposes.

ABANDONED BY THE GUARDS

"This is the twilight of the gods. There is utter consternation in Itter Castle, our prison. All the radios have been locked up in the Commandant's office for the last few days, probably to keep the garrison's morale from caving in, but in spite of all the precautions, disastrous news reports continue to filter through. . . .

"An officer arrived sometime during the night, a relative of the castle warden. He has difficulty getting around on his two canes, the result of wounds sustained on the Russian front. He has been assigned to the quartermaster corps. He arrived in so frenzied a state that all the soldiers were soon buzzing around him. He had just returned from a mission to Prague, where he had found the situation extremely tense. The Gestapo were on edge and unable to keep up with events. The cafes and all other public establishments had shut down. In short, Prague was a city on the verge of revolting against its oppressor. The SS were deeply stirred by the grim images conjured up by this disabled veteran, now convinced that two years ago his blood had dappled the snows of Russia to no purpose at all.

"This morning, as I was cautiously making my way over the ice-covered ground, I could see dejection on the faces of the sentinels and consternation in the eyes of the soldiers as they busily went about their chores, as they do every day. . . . *The young Czech who waits on the SS and hears and sees everything told me that we had to be on our guard.* Some of the SS were talking about suicide. Others planned to seize all the food supplies, drink all the beer and the few bottles of wine that are kept in the cellar, get drunk, and shoot us. The two faces of Germany."[7]

So an anxious Edouard Daladier wrote in his diary in early 1945. By late April, the desperation of the SS guards at Castle Itter had grown even more anxious. The camp commandant, SS Captain Sebastian Wimmer was, by nature, a brutish and cruel man. He had tortured prisoners at Dachau with no visible remorse and was given to drunken bouts of ranting and raging when given bad news. He was a tyrant with respect to the "numbered prisoners" (those who weren't VIPs) but treated the French honor prisoners with grudging respect and courtesy, something expected of him by the Gestapo. It was his hope that after the war the French would speak positively of him, since all officers in the SS were considered de facto war criminals whenever they were captured by the Allies. Wimmer's family was stationed with him at Castle Itter, which added to his anxiety; he was anxious to keep them alive. Wimmer and the guards under his command, likely within days of being captured by the Americans, were loath to kill the French prisoners under their care despite Heinrich Himmler's orders.

By late April the situation was desperate. Roving bands of German SS and Wehrmacht troops were roaming the countryside in front of the American advances into Austria. Some were looting and killing, others were simply trying to hide out until they could surrender to the Americans. On April 30th, SS Lieutenant Colonel Wilhelm Weiter arrived at the castle with a few guards and his family. He had been the last commandant of the Dachau prison camp and was now trying to escape from the Allies. A cruel man, he bragged to Wimmer and the French honor prisoners that his last order at Dachau had been killing 2,000 prisoners. This alarmed the French, of course, who feared that he was there to do the same to them. However, early the next morning two gunshots were heard from his room in the castle. When the door was forced open, they found that Weiter had committed suicide, first shooting himself in the stomach and, when that failed, in the head. Weiter's suicide unnerved Wimmer, who now feared the worst for his own capture and imprisonment.

On May 3, 1945, Wimmer ordered Zvonimir Cuckovic, a Croatian and "numbered" prisoner, to travel to a nearby town to connect the electricity and otherwise prepare a home that Wimmer had found for he and his family to live in. Wimmer's hope was to avoid the advancing Americans by essentially disappearing into the civilian population.

What he did not know is that Cuckovic, in collaboration with the French honor prisoners, instead made his way through German lines to the American forces in Innsbruck. He carried a note from the French, written in English, requesting assistance in liberating the castle and protecting the prisoners.

When Cuckovic failed to return, Wimmer panicked. He and his family departed the castle before first light on the morning of May 4th. The other German guards used this as an opportunity to escape as well, leaving the prisoners completely unprotected. Clemenceau and Reynaud walked unmolested into the village of Itter, but quickly returned to the castle when they saw hostile German soldiers in the town.

Now completely vulnerable, the French honor prisoners met together and decided on three courses of action. They would fly a French tricolor flag from one of the high castle windows to prevent an Allied air attack; request that Kurt-Siegfried Schrader, a disabled SS officer who had retired and lived in the village of Itter, move to the castle to offer his protection and negotiate on behalf of the prisoners when approached by hostile Germans; and then send a second emissary to the Americans since it was assumed that Cuckovic had been captured or killed. Another numbered prisoner, Andreas Krobot, a Czech citizen and castle cook, agreed to undertake this mission.

Additionally, the prisoners broke into the castle's arms locker and took possession of the various weapons left behind by the departed guards. While most of the prisoners were in their sixties or seventies, most had served in World War I and had combat experience. They were willing to fight for their lives, if necessary.

RESCUE OPERATIONS GET UNDERWAY

Rescue operation #1—Kurt Schrader accepts command of Castle Itter

Though not decisive in the long run, it had great psychic value to the prisoners when their delegation to SS Captain Kurt Schrader met with success. Schrader agreed to move, with his family, to the castle and to help the French set up their defenses, as well as to negotiate with any SS-units to protect the French.[8]

Rescue operation #2—Andreas Krobot connects with German Major Sepp Gangl

Krobot used a bicycle to leave the castle and make his way into the nearby town of Wörgl using backstreets. When he arrived there, he had no idea how to find the Americans, so he took a chance and reached out to an Austrian. Fortunately, the person he contacted was part of the resistance effort and he immediately took Krobot to see German Major Josef "Sepp" Gangl, a Wehrmacht officer who had earlier decided to defect and who had reached out to the Austrian Alois Mayr resistance cell, offering to help protect Austrians from the SS when they reached Wörgl.

When Major Gangl heard of the Itter prisoners' predicament he made a quick and crucial decision—he would surrender the town of Wörgl to the Americans immediately, freeing up American troops to help effect a rescue of Castle Itter. He enlisted a driver to take him the seven miles to the nearest American command center in the town of Kufstein, an extremely dangerous journey since he had to fly a white flag to prevent the Americans from shooting, but knew that the flag would also signal to any SS troops in the area that he was betraying Germany, attracting their hostility.

When Gangl arrived in Kufstein the town seemed deserted until he rounded a corner and came face-to-face with four American M-4 Sherman tanks! Gangl and his driver stepped slowly out of their *kubelwagen* (a German Army jeep) with their hands raised above their heads, the white flag fluttering in the breeze, and waited while American sentries approached them. They knelt on their knees when instructed, fearing that they would be executed on the spot. But the Americans simply frisked them and had them stand so they could go to meet the officer in charge.

Captain Jack Lee listened as Gangl, speaking in halting English, offered to surrender the town of Wörgl to the Americans. Gangl told Captain Lee that he had important information about high profile French prisoners in need of rescue at Castle Itter. Lee allowed Gangl to hand him the note written by Christine Mabire requesting assistance.

Without a word, Captain Jack Lee hopped onto the Sherman tank, dropped down through the turret, and was out of sight for several minutes. When he reappeared, he smiled at Major Gangl and said, "It looks like we're all going on a rescue mission!" He had been in contact with his superiors by radio, who had authorized the mission.

Captain Lee assumed personal command of the rescue, which was consistent with his courageous leadership in previous battles. Just two weeks earlier he had been awarded the Bronze Star at the battle of Strasbourg for "superior leadership ability, cool and aggressive handling of the platoon, and his courage and his ability to meet any situation that confronted him."[9] He was about to be confronted by a situation unlike any other in World War II.

Rescue operation #3—Cuckovic connects with Major John Kramers

Though no longer in communication with the French prisoners, the electrician Zvonimir Cuckovic was still very much in the picture. He had ridden his bicycle more than fifty miles through German-held territory to reach Innsbruck. When stopped along the way he would display a note he had from Commandant Wimmer, authorizing him to travel to work on the electricity of his house, which was accepted as proof of passage. When he finally arrived in Innsbruck, he went to the American lines where he was presented to Major John T. Kramers. Cuckovic gave Kramers the note he had been given by the French prisoners, which read:

"'The American military authorities are hereby informed that the undernamed fourteen French statesmen, generals, ladies and personalities are confined in the castle of Itter. The village and castle of Itter are eight kilometers east of Wörgl. The prisoners are Edouard Daladier and Paul Reynaud, former prime ministers of France. General Gamelin, former commander in chief of the French army. Leon Jouhaux, secretary of the Confederation General du Travail. Mme Alfred Cailliau, sister of General de Gaulle and her husband. Michel Clemenceau, son of the French statesman, Colonel de la Roque, chief of the Croix de Feu organization, Jean Borotra, ex-Minister of Sports in the Vichy cabinet, M. Granger, a relative of General Giraud, General Weygand and his wife. Mme Brucklin, secretary of Leon Jouhoux. Mme Mabire, secretary of Paul Reynaud.'

"'How did you manage to get out of the place?' Major Kramers asked Cuckovic. 'Why, the commander sent me out.'

'What commander? The German commander?'

'Yes, the German commander. You see, he is responsible for the safety of these important people, and he is afraid the SS might shoot his prisoners at the last minute. So, he hopes the American will come quickly.'"[10]

War correspondent Meyer Levin was embedded with Kramers's group and accompanied them on this mission. His firsthand account continues:

"So the next morning a task force set out. It was composed of four tank destroyers, several jeeps, a truckload of soldiers to deal with SS men who didn't know there was an armistice on, and an empty truck for the trunks and baggage of the personalities.

"We romped along a fine road lined with cheering Polish, Czechs, French and Russian ex-slaves and ex-prisoners who here, as everywhere, seemed to have sprung up out of the ground the instant the wind of liberation blew their way. It was a fine warm day and the mountain scenery was first class and we had a fine tourist ride for some twenty miles on the road to Wörgl. Then, at a crossroad, a bunch of Austrian partisans waved us down. Breathlessly, they described a brush they had had with SS men, farther up this road. . . .

"Our little party paused for reflection. There we were, alone in what was still [German-occupied territory]. Liberating a castle full of big names was important, but it was also important not to get killed in so doing, especially on the day when fighting was supposed to have stopped. To add point to the argument, there came a familiar whine [of artillery], which we thought we had already heard for the last time. Then the blast, and 100 yards away there was a black burst.

"The boys in the tanks promptly backed among some trees for cover. The soldiers hopped off their truck, took positions in a ditch, and watched the shells come down.

"'They seen us.'

"'If they're shooting for us, that's lousy poor shooting.'

"'Yeah, but it's eighty-eights [88-millimeter anti-tank cannons] and they got observation on this road.'

"Major Kramers made a swift [reconnaissance] up the road, did some radio talk with headquarters, and decided we couldn't clear the road to Itter without help."[11]

The rescue of Castle Itter was getting more complicated.

THE BATTLE FOR CASTLE ITTER

As the closest American force to Itter, Captain Jack Lee agreed to the rescue operation, but decided on a reconnaissance mission first. Riding in Major Gangl's military vehicle (so hostile Germans wouldn't shoot them), they made their way to Wörgl, where Captain Lee formally accepted Major Sepp Gangl's surrender of the town. In a highly unusual move, he allowed the Germans to keep their arms since they were now allied in the forthcoming battle for Castle Itter. His resources stretched thin, Lee also allowed the Austrians to administer their town until other Americans arrived, while charging Gangl's Germans with its security. The Germans under Gangl's command were now American allies—but this duty required Gangl to leave many of his loyal troops in Wörgl rather than proceeding to the castle.

The reconnaissance mission continued to the castle where, after a few brushes with hostile German troops on the narrow road out of the castle, they arrived to the great relief of the castle inhabitants. Lee assumed command of the castle's defenses from retired SS Captain Schrader, who promised that he would stay on to help in the fight.

Lee headed back to his unit at Kufstein to organize the rescue. Unfortunately, only two tanks were available, but he was determined to proceed. Lee took command of one tank and his second-in-command Harry Basse the other. On the way back to Wörgl he commandeered an additional five Sherman tanks from the 753rd Tank Battalion, also persuading Colonel George Lynch of the 142nd Infantry Regiment to assign him three squads of infantrymen. Lynch promised to follow Lee's force as soon as possible.

All went well until they reached an old bridge on the way to Wörgl. Only four tanks made it over the bridge before it collapsed under the immense weight of the tanks (66,000 pounds each). The others could not make it across the river, so they returned to Kufstein. When he reached Wörgl, Major Gangl asked if he would leave two of the Shermans to defend the town, offering to send more of his German troops to the castle. Lee agreed to this, and then set out for the castle with just two Sherman tanks, fourteen American soldiers, a German *kubelwagen* and a small Mercedes truck carrying ten German soldiers—all under the command of a United States Army captain.

When the group reached the village of Itter they encountered hostile fire from SS troops. They were able to push past this to a small bridge that had been wired with explosives by the SS. Lee took his own tank across but decided to leave the other at the bridge to protect it, since it was the only way for the group to retreat after rescuing the prisoners in the castle. The men he left at the bridge proceeded to remove the demolition charges.

Having started out with a force of seven tanks, Lee finally reached the castle with just one. Even though it was late, he took time to carefully turn his tank around and back it up the ever-narrowing road so that it would face forward against an SS advance.

Once inside the castle, Lee went to work quickly, organizing its defense even as hostile German units had started firing on the outer walls. Originally, he had planned to evacuate the prisoners and personnel immediately. Now it was decided that it was safer to remain in the castle behind its thick masonry walls while waiting for other American units to arrive. Situated in a steep gorge, the castle was difficult for the attackers to reach and the turrets provided opportunities to shoot down at any Germans attempting to scale the outer walls.

Captain Lee's first order was for the French to move to the cellar so they would be protected. This was met with protests by the aged warriors who said they would much rather die fighting on the castle walls than being holed up in a cellar. But Lee reminded them that he was in command and that they would be of no use to the French people if they died needlessly at Castle Itter.

His next move was to meet with his leadership team. Captain Lee divided the Germans into three defensive groups and directed them to various locations on the walls of the castle to respond to attacks as they developed. Germans now loyal to the Americans were instructed to wear dark armbands so they could be distinguished from hostile forces.

At four o'clock in the morning on May 5th, the hostile German attack began. First came brief lunges toward the castle by the Waffen-SS to identify vulnerabilities in the defenses. The SS successfully penetrated the barbed-wire perimeter and a number made it to the base of the castle walls by sunrise. Edouard Daladier was nearly killed by enemy fire because he had disregarded Lee's orders and was taking a walk in the courtyard. Observers in the upper turret of the castle next spotted a 20mm antiaircraft cannon and an 88mm cannon being positioned to fire on the castle, as well as German transport trucks carrying 150 SS troops from the 17th SS Panzer-Grenadier Division. These were crack troops experienced with small-arms fire and hand grenades.

Shortly after this, Lee received even more disturbing news. One of the Germans under Sepp Gangl's command had deserted the castle, presumably going over to the enemy. This was potentially devastating since he had inside knowledge of the defensive arrangements of the castle, including troop positioning and the scarce number of defenders relative to the attackers. Captain Lee was furious that none of the other Germans under Gangl's command had fired on this deserter and he questioned Gangl whether others were planning on deserting as well. Gangl convinced him that they were all loyal and would obey Lee's orders.

The situation was frantic—Lee's radio had stopped working and there were none available in the castle. They desperately needed reinforcements before the real attack started, but it appeared that there was no way to reach out. But then one of the numbered prisoners suggested that they use the castle telephone to call into Wörgl. Incredulous that a telephone was still working in a battle zone, Lee picked up the handset and found that it worked. He was soon connected to the Wörgl City Hall and urgently requested help from the Austrian resistance cells. Word went out, and three men started toward the castle immediately while others were collecting. At this point Lee still had no idea that American Major Kramers was on his way to the castle, though not as fast as he'd hoped since he was slowed by administrative orders, hostile Nazi fire, and by the mechanics of making it through a road clogged with German troops wanting to surrender.

HOSTILITIES BEGIN

At 10:10 A.M. many of the French prisoners were out in the courtyard in defiance of Lee's order. Their complacency ended abruptly when an 88mm round slammed into the third floor of the castle, destroying what had been Maurice Gamelin's room. Rubble showered down on the French in the courtyard just as the 20mm cannon started firing into the tower as well. Rifles were fired from the opposite hillsides, sending bullets thudding into the castle walls. The French prisoners were quickly cowed as Lee shouted at them to leave the courtyard.

Just a few moments after the firing began, an antitank shell slammed into the tank parked in front of the castle. The projectile penetrated the thick armor of the Sherman tank and ricocheted inside the cabin, sending up flames from the engine grill. Somehow the tank driver was able to escape through the hatch just moments before the fuel tanks exploded, which in turn ignited all the ammunition. In a matter of moments, the tank was a raging inferno parked directly in front of the castle. The dazed driver managed to duck down on the side of the embankment and ran in a crouched position with SS troops shooting at him as he made his way to the castle entrance. Now all that was left to the defenders was small arms fire.

At this point the French prisoners insisted on joining the fight, and they moved to reinforce the Germans and Americans firing down on the German infantry while doing their best to avoid being killed by the cannons firing at them.

It was in this moment that one of the prisoners, Paul Reynaud, caused the first casualty of the battle. Rather than crouch while moving to his position, Reynaud walked upright—in direct line of sight to the attackers outside. Seeing this, Major Gangl ran to shove him down, but was struck by a hostile bullet while doing so. He collapsed and died on the spot.

Realizing that their only hope of survival was to bring whatever American troops were in the area to the castle, tennis player Jean Borotra volunteered to run for help. To do so he had to make his way out of the castle, ford a cold stream, and run the back roads into Itter to avoid hostile German troops. Running several miles as quickly as he could, he finally connected with American Colonel Lynch, who recognized the urgency of the situation and authorized Borotra to lead an attack group back to the castle. Borotra insisted that he be given an American uniform and gun, which proved useful on his return to the castle as he managed to shoot several SS troops attacking the rescue force. His group also took twelve SS troops prisoner without suffering any casualties.

Even better, Major Kramers had finally reached Wörgl, where he called the castle by telephone. Lee told him that they were still holding out, but that they were very nearly out of ammunition. Kramers quickly enlisted the help of six M4 Shermans from the 753rd Tank Battalion and several half-tracks with men from the 142nd Infantry's Company E to join him in a rush to the castle. They were frustrated as they did so by exultant Austrians who came out to celebrate, often trying to throw themselves at the tanks to hug their liberators. The road was also clogged with German soldiers wishing to surrender, including some sixteen-year-olds who claimed they'd never fired a gun. But despite these obstacles, Kramers's force made progress, eventually knocking out the heavy German guns firing on the castle and sending German troops fleeing into the hills with a sustained attack with the tanks' .30-caliber machine guns. When all the American tanks arrived at Castle Itter, where Captain Lee's tank was still burning, the SS attackers fled, and the battle was won! Upon entering the castle,

Kramers discovered that the defenders had run completely out of ammunition and were essentially defenseless.

PRISONERS NO MORE

The joy inside the castle as all the groups involved in the rescue converged in the courtyard was overwhelming! As war photographer Eric Schwab entered the courtyard, Edouard Daladier rushed up and kissed him on both his cheeks. Michel Clemenceau slapped Cuckovic on the back and thanked him for his courage in finding the Americans. Military correspondent Meyer Levin started interviewing the prisoners to capture their intriguing stories, and was touched when Alfred Cailliau told of his experience of being stripped naked in the middle of the coldest winter on record, then forced to ride on a train to Buchenwald for three days without food or clothing. His wife said that she had been forced to sleep in the open, with nothing more than straw while on the way to Itter. Reynaud related that he had spent months alone in solitary confinement in the prison at Oranienburg.

All the prisoner's had stories to tell. But as they did so, the old bitterness and rivalries revealed themselves to the point that Major Kramers observed that "some of these people were as happy to be liberated from each other's company as they were to be liberated from imprisonment!"[12]

Now safely in Allied hands, the prisoners rushed upstairs to pack their belongings, their heavy trunks loaded on a cargo truck, in preparation to depart for Innsbruck.

"We all moved down toward the tanks and the automobiles. The people from the village had gathered in the town square. Austrian flags were hanging from the windows. An old antiques dealer from Berlin, who had taken refuge in the area with his daughter, told us, 'We have been liberated too.' I noticed that Resistance fighters from Wörgl were there as well.

"At 7 P.M. we headed down to Innsbruck, free at last. We were shown to the command post of the general leading the 103rd Division, Anthony McAuliffe. That was the heroic division that had been surrounded in Bastogne. The general had in fact been on leave at the time, in the United States. He immediately had himself flown back and parachuted into the middle of his troops. His encircled division eventually broke out. He greeted us in princely, kindly fashion and honored us with a candlelight dinner in his Tirolean villa."[13]

After a night of celebration, they separated into groups based on their political persuasions and then were transported to Augsburg, Germany, where they dined with Seventh Army Commander Alexander Patch.

The next day, they were taken to the French First Army headquarters commanded by Jean de Lattre de Tassigny. He ordered that Weygand, Borotra, and de La Rocque be separated from the others so they could be placed on trial for collaborationist activities related to their service to the Vichy regime of Philippe Pétain. The others flew to Paris on General Charles de Gaulle's personal airplane.

The Germans who assisted in the rescue of the castle were sent to a prisoner-of-war camp for processing, but with special recognition for their help in saving the French. The numbered prisoners were returned safely to their home countries, including Zvonimir Cuckovic and Andreas Krobot who were instrumental in the rescue.

Captain Jack Lee was awarded the Distinguished Service Cross for his leadership in the defense of Castle Itter. His citation noted his "extraordinary heroism in action, as Commanding Officer of Company B, 23rd Tank Battalion, in the vicinity of Wörgl, Austria, and the Itter Castle on 4–5 May 1945. Captain Lee, with a small group of soldiers infiltrated into hostile territory, demoralized enemy forces, prevented the destruction of two key bridges, and caused 200 German soldiers to surrender.

"He found many prominent French prisoners at Itter Castle,

and immediately organized a defense with both American and German troops. Despite a fanatical SS attack and heavy artillery barrage, Captain Lee's men held until friendly troops arrived.

"Captain Lee's initiative, boldness, courage, resourcefulness and outstanding qualities of leadership exemplify the highest traditions of the Army and the United States."[14]

The fourteen French honor prisoners returned to their lives. Weygand and Reynaud reentered politics, with Reynaud elected to the National Assembly as well as serving in several cabinet positions. Leon Jouhaux and August Bruchlen, the labor leaders, were awarded the 1951 Nobel Peace Prize as well as other notable honors for their postwar activities. The trials of the collaborationists never came about and they all returned to their lives. Tennis player Jean Borotra was as popular as ever and returned to his successful business ventures as well as serving as an officer of the French Lawn Tennis Association. He competed in seniors tournaments well into his nineties.

As for Josef Gangl, the SS officer turned ally and the only person killed in the defense of Castle Itter, he is considered an Austrian national hero with a street named after him in Wörgl. He is interred in the Wörgl city cemetery next to a memorial in his honor for his defense of the city and the castle on May 5, 1945.

WHY THEY FOUGHT?

I started this book responding to the question, "Why do you write about war?" The answer is that the people featured in these stories deserve to be remembered for their courage and sacrifice. But the question remains: "Why did they fight?" As you have seen, except for some who served in the Ghost Army, the people featured in this book were not *required* to fight, but they volunteered to do so even at the risk of death or torture. Some of the scenes that stand out so vividly to me include

Virginia Hall climbing through the snowbound passes of the Pyrenees mountains, fleeing at literally the last moment before Klaus Barbie could catch her—with an artificial leg that bled at the stump because the crossing was so difficult. Yet when she arrived in Spain, she immediately agitated to be sent back to France to continue the fight. It is gratifying that she has a permanent exhibit in the CIA museum, because she risked everything to help the Allies win World War II.

William Sebold secretly working with the FBI to deceive Germany, knowing that if the connection were discovered, German agents in the United States would kill him. Even more, he knew that his family back in Germany were also at risk. But because he recognized that America was on the right side of the battle, he would fulfill his oath of allegiance no matter the cost.

Marlene Dietrich—wow!—the beautiful Hollywood star who could have waited out the war in luxury instead going to the front lines to entertain soldiers, and also secretly recording radio messages and songs to demoralize German soldiers, an act that put a price on her head. But she had lived in both Germany and America, and she recognized the evil of Nazi rule and fought with the gifts she had to end their dominance in her native land.

My view of **Juan Pujol** may be different than some, since I have written and published ten novels, accounts that required me to create hundreds of characters in far-flung locations. It is *hard* to keep track of everything to assure consistency from beginning to end. I've never had the threat of assassination hanging over my head if I made a mistake. But that was both the task and the risk Pujol set out for himself—creating a world filled with imaginary informants that saved *tens of thousands* in the real world. Amazing!

Carl Lutz is my personal hero. Quiet and introverted, he saved 72,000 Jewish lives when everyone in power wanted him to do otherwise. I cannot fully imagine the emotional pressure he endured —and today hundreds of thousands are alive because of his courage.

The Ghost Army seemed quirky to me because it involved highly creative people—artists, actors, and engineers—working in a highly destructive environment. The risk to their lives was *very* real when a handful of ghost soldiers stood in a seventy-mile gap in the lines, receiving the brunt of German artillery to draw that fire away from combat troops.

The defense of **Castle Itter** showed the mettle of combatants on both sides. The war was officially over, but both Germans and Americans rushed to the defense of French prisoners. Neither side had an obligation, but both had a willingness to help.

The bottom line is that these people acted on the principles that evil should be resisted and that freedom is worth dying for. *Why We Fought?* Because it was the right thing to do.

—Jerry Borrowman

NOTES

Chapter 1—Virginia Hall: "We Must Find and Destroy Her"

1. Report on the Heckler Circuit.
2. See Purcell, *Woman of No Importance*, 16.
3. Pearson, *Wolves at the Door*, location 374 of 4133.
4. See Pearson, *Wolves at the Door*, location 551.
5. Pearson, *Wolves at the Door*, location 1024.
6. Purcell, *Woman of No Importance*, 77.
7. Purcell, *Woman of No Importance*, 91.
8. Churchill, *Duel of Wits*, 83–84.
9. Churchill, *Duel of Wits*, 80; paragraphing altered.
10. Churchill, *Duel of Wits*, 91–92.
11. Churchill, *Duel of Wits*, 97; paragraphing altered.
12. Pearson, *Wolves at the Door*, location 2879.
13. Pearson, *Wolves at the Door*, locations 2640–49; emphasis added.
14. After defeating Soviet troops in the Crimea, the Germans conscripted many prisoners into their own units and sent them to France in advance of the Allied invasion. These troops were from the Tatar regions and had little loyalty to the Germans.
15. Report on the Heckler Circuit.
16. Report on the Heckler Circuit.
17. Memorandum for the President.

Chapter 2—William Sebold and Sabotage in America

1. US Bureau of Labor Statistics; available at https://www.bls.gov/data/inflation_calculator.htm; accessed July 8, 2020.
2. See Hynd, *Passport to Treason*, 194–95.
3. A "fifth column" identifies a small group of people within a much larger population who work to undermine the larger group, usually in service of an enemy group or nation. The phrase is attributed to a Nationalist general in the Spanish Civil War, Emilio Mola Vidal, who said that as his

four military columns moved toward Madrid, his fifth column of militant supporters within the city would rise up to support the military. See "Fifth Column," *Encylopaedia Brittanica*.

4. Naturalization Oath of Allegiance to the United States of America.
5. See Duffy, *Double Agent*, 59–64.
6. Duffy, *Double Agent*, 113–14.
7. Hynd, *Passport to Treason*, 29–30.
8. Hynd, *Passport to Treason*, 42–44.
9. Hynd, *Passport to Treason*, 48.
10. Hynd, *Passport to Treason*, 56.
11. Hynd, *Passport to Treason*, 113.
12. Hynd, *Passport to Treason*, 134–36.
13. Hynd, *Passport to Treason*, 166–67.
14. Hynd, *Passport to Treason*, 168.
15. Duffy, *Double Agent*, 147, 148.
16. Hynd, *Passport to Treason*, 209.
17. "Famous Cases and Criminals: Duquesne Spy Ring."
18. Duffy, *Double Agent*, 231, 232–33.
19. See Duffy, *Double Agent*, 256.
20. Duffy, *Double Agent*, 280.
21. Duffy, *Double Agent*, 281.

Chapter 3—Marlene Dietrich: Hollywood Actor Spies on the Nazis

1. Riva, *Marlene Dietrich*, 56.
2. Cited in Wieland, *Dietrich and Riefenstahl*, 352.
3. Wieland, *Dietrich and Riefenstahl*, 561fn21; citing the original identification card, which is on display in the Marlene Dietrich collection, Filmmuseum, Berlin, Germany.
4. Liebovitz and Miller, *Lili Marlene*.
5. Riva, *Marlene Dietrich*, locations 10269–10284.
6. See Wieland, *Dietrich and Riefenstahl*, 366.
7. Wieland, *Dietrich and Riefenstahl*, 369.

Chapter 4—Juan Pujol: The Allies' Most Successful Double Agent

1. Talty, *Agent Garbo*, xv.
2. Pujol and West, *Operation Garbo*, location 197 of 4709.
3. Pujol and West, *Operation Garbo*, location 197.
4. Pujol and West, *Operation Garbo*, locations 497–593.
5. Pujol and West, *Operation Garbo*, location 611.

6. Talty, *Agent Garbo*, 31.
7. Pujol and West, *Operation Garbo*, locations 1143–1169.
8. Talty, *Agent Garbo*, 84.
9. Talty, *Agent Garbo*, 93–95; emphasis added.
10. Pujol and West, *Operation Garbo*, location 2442.
11. Pujol and West, *Operation Garbo*, location 2442.
12. Pujol and West, *Operation Garbo*, location 2529.
13. Pujol and West, *Operation Garbo*, location 3609.
14. Pujol and West, *Operation Garbo*, location 3339.

Chapter 5—Carl Lutz Saves 72,000 Jewish Lives

1. Tschuy, *Dangerous Diplomacy*, 24.
2. Grunwald-Spier, *Other Schindlers*, location 642.
3. Tschuy, *Dangerous Diplomacy*, 29.
4. Tschuy, *Dangerous Diplomacy*, 33.
5. Budapest consists of the formerly consolidated cities of Buda and Pest, separated from each other by the Danube River.
6. "The Holocaust: The Vrba-Wetzler Report (Auschwitz Protocols)."
7. Tschuy, *Dangerous Diplomacy*, 87–88.
8. Lutz, "The Rescue Work of a Swiss in World War II," 5–8; cited in Grunwald-Spier, *Other Schindlers*, location 651.
9. Winston Churchill, "Winston Churchill's The Second World War and the Holocaust's Uniqueness."
10. Tschuy, *Dangerous Diplomacy*, 182–83.
11. Agnes Hirschi, stepdaughter of Carl Lutz, in an email to Agnes Grunwald-Spier in March 2001. Cited in Grunwald-Spier, *Other Schindlers*, location 683.

Chapter 6—The Ghost Army

1. Fox, Official History of the 23rd Headquarters Special Troops.
2. Machiavelli, *Discourses on Livy*.
3. Sun Tzu, *The Art of War*.
4. Gerry and Janet Souter, *Ghost Army*, location 609.
5. Gerry and Janet Souter, *Ghost Army*, location 519.
6. Gerry and Janet Souter, *Ghost Army*, location 1261
7. Fox, Official History of the 23rd Headquarters Special Troops.
8. Fox, Official History of the 23rd Headquarters Special Troops.
9. Fox, Official History of the 23rd Headquarters Special Troops.
10. A detailed description of the heroism displayed by combat engineers

bridging the Rhine is included in Jerry Borrowman, *Invisible Heroes of World War II* (Shadow Mountain, 2019).

11. Fox, Official History of the 23rd Headquarters Special Troops.
12. Fox, Official History of the 23rd Headquarters Special Troops.
13. Fox, Official History of the 23rd Headquarters Special Troops.

Chapter 7—The Battle for Castle Itter

1. Piekalkiewicz, *Secret Agents, Spies, and Saboteurs*, 520–21.
2. Harding, *Last Battle*, 5–10.
3. Daladier, *Prison Journal 1940–1945*, 273.
4. Levin, "We Liberated Who's Who," 97.
5. Vichy was made the capital of the unoccupied areas of France following the fall of Paris. The Nazis had direct control in occupied France and the Pétain government in Vichy had semiautonomous governing powers in unoccupied France. With the Germans always on their doorsteps, Pétain's government cooperated extensively with the Germans. Eventually, German troops moved into the unoccupied areas after America attacked the German forces in North Africa.
6. Harding, *Last Battle*, 54.
7. Daladier, *Prison Journal 1940–1945*, 317–18.
8. In his July 28, 1945, article in the *Saturday Evening Post*, journalist Meyer Levin indicated that the request to Kurt Schrader actually came from German Commandant Wimmer prior to his escape from the castle. In his extensively researched book *The Last Battle*, author Stephen Harding indicates that it was a delegation from the French. Either way, Schrader was at the castle helping actively in its defense.
9. General Orders 33, HQs 12th Armored Division April 19, 1945; cited in Harding, *Last Battle*, 118.
10. Levin, "We Liberated Who's Who," 97.
11. Levin, "We Liberated Who's Who," 17, 97.
12. Levin, "We Liberated Who's Who," 97.
13. Daladier, *Prison Journal 1940–1945*, 339.
14. Cited in Harding, *Last Battle*, 165.

BIBLIOGRAPHY

Beyer, Rick, and Elizabeth Sayles. *The Ghost Army of World War II*. 2015. Kindle Edition.

Bourne-Patterson, Robert. *SOE Operations in France 1941–1945, An Official Account of the Special Operations Executive's French Circuits*. 1946. Reprint, 2016.

Churchill, Peter. *Duel of Wits*. 1953.

Daladier, Edouard. *Prison Journal 1940–1945*. 1995.

Duffy, Peter. *Double Agent: The First Hero of World War II and How the FBI Outwitted and Destroyed a Nazi Spy Ring*. 2014. Kindle Edition.

"Famous Cases and Criminals: Duquesne Spy Ring." *FBI.gov* (website). Available at https://www.fbi.gov/history/famous-cases/duquesne-spy-ring; accessed July 16, 2020.

"Fifth Column." *Encylopaedia Britannica*. Available at https://www.britannica.com/topic/fifth-column; accessed July 8, 2020.

Fox, Fred. *Official History of the 23rd Headquarters Special Troops*. 1945. Declassified by the United States Army in 1966. National Archives II, College Park, Maryland. Record Group 407, SPHQ-23; Entry 427— WWII, Stock Area 270, Row 64, Compartment 24, Shelf 6, Boxes 18481–83.

Gralley, Craig R. "A Climb to Freedom: A Personal Journey in Virginia Hall's Steps." *Studies in Intelligence*, Vol. 61 No. 1. Central Intelligence Agency. Available at https://www.cia.gov/resources/csi/studies-in-intelligence/volume-61-no-1/a-climb-to-freedom-a-personal-journey-in-virginia-halls-steps/; accessed 18 April 2020.

Grunwald-Spier, Agnes. *Other Schindlers: Why Some People Chose to Save Jews in the Holocaust*. 2011. Kindle Edition.

Harding, Stephen. *The Last Battle: When US and German Soldiers Joined Forces in the Waning Hours of World War II*. 2013.

"The Holocaust: The Vrba-Wetzler Report (Auschwitz Protocols)." *Jewish Virtual Library* (website). Available at https://www.jewishvirtuallibrary.org/the-vrba-wetzler-report-auschwitz-protocols; accessed October 22, 2020.

Hynd, Alan. *Passport to Treason: The Inside Story of Spies in America.* 1943. Reprint.

Levin, Meyer. "We Liberated Who's Who." *Saturday Evening Post*, Vol. 218, No. 3. (July 21, 1945).

Liebovitz, Liel, and Matthew Miller. *Lili Marlene: The Soldiers' Song of World War II.* 2008.

Lutz, Charles R. (Carl). "The Rescue Work of a Swiss in World War II." In *Neue Zuercher Zeitung* (NZZ), No. 2464 (30 June 1961): 5–8.

Memorandum for the President from William J Donovan Regarding Distinguished Service Cross (DSC) Award to Virginia Hall, 12 May 1945. National Archives. Available at https://catalog.archives.gov/id/595672; accessed 16 March 2021.

"Naturalization Oath of Allegiance to the United States of America." US Citizenship and Immigration Services (website). Available at https://www.uscis.gov/us-citizenship/naturalization-test/naturalization-oath-allegiance-united-states-america; accessed July 8, 2020.

Paldiel, Mordecai. *Diplomat Heroes of the Holocaust.* 2007.

Pearson, Judith L. *The Wolves at the Door: The True Story of America's Greatest Female Spy.* 2008.

Piekalkiewicz, Janusz. *Secret Agents, Spies and Saboteurs: Famous Undercover Missions of World War II.* 1969.

Pujol, Juan Garcia, and Nigel West. *Operation Garbo: The Personal Story of the Most Successful Spy of World War II.* 2011. Kindle Edition.

Purnell, Sonia. *A Woman of No Importance: The Untold Story of the American Spy Who Helped Win World War II.* 2019.

Report on the Heckler Circuit; Virginia Hall; Office of Strategic Services; Volume 3; July, August, September 1944; F-Section; Western Europe. Available at 801492.org/Air%20Crew/Ewart/Saint-Heckler%20Reports.pdf; accessed 18 April 2020.

Riva, Maria. *Marlene Dietrich: The Life.* 2017.

Souter, Gerry and Janet. *The Ghost Army: Conning the Third Reich.* 2019. Kindle Edition.

Talty, Stephen. *Agent Garbo: The Brilliant, Eccentric Secret Agent Who Tricked Hitler and Saved D-Day.* 2012.

Tschuy, Theo. *Dangerous Diplomacy: The Story of Carl Lutz, Rescuer of 62,000 Hungarian Jews.* 2000.

Wieland, Karin. *Dietrich and Riefenstahl: Hollywood, Berlin, and a Century in Two Lives.* 2015.

INDEX